WEST HAM 'TILL I DIE

WEST HAM 'TILL I DIE

BOLEYN BOOKS

Published October 2000 by
Boleyn Books
Tel: (01708) 379877

Printed by Cox & Wyman Ltd,
Cardiff Road, Reading, Berkshire, RG1 8EX.

Distributed by Vine House Distribution Ltd,
Waldenbury, North Common, Challey, East Sussex,
BN8 4DR, England.
Tel: (01825) 723398
Email: sales@vinehouseuk.co.uk

Set in Helvetica Roman

ISBN 0 9529641 1 2

Front cover photograph of Robert Banks with
Hammerettes Jerrie-Lee and Kerrie-Ann by Tim
Hetherington

For Chloe

ACKNOWLEDGEMENTS

Loads of people I would like to thank for their help and support:

Bob and Mary Banks, Lynn Cooper and Sylvia Prior – for being the most supportive family I could wish for.

Kevin Williamson – for being a top mate.

Mark Crowther – a good friend and tolerant landlord.

Stuart, Jill and Callum Davies; Mike, Nicola and John McManus – for always being there.

Dr. George Sik – for his constant encouragement.

Gary Firmager – for his unerring confidence in my ability.

Boleyn Books – for showing faith in me.

Fabiana Dixon – for her friendship.

Chris Maflin, Henry Perales, Alan Porter, Roger Newman and Tony Marsh at CIS – for being supportive managers and never asking where I disappeared to on a Wednesday afternoon.

If I have missed anyone, I apologise – you all played your part. Thank you.

The publishers would also like to thank:

Cliff Moulder and Bradley Marks at M. Press (Sales) Ltd, Peter Stewart, Carl Bailey and the front cover girls, Danny Francis, Kelly Harkins, Richard Squibb and all at Vine Distribution Ltd.

FOREWORD
By GARY FIRMAGER
Editor, *Over Land And Sea*

I am delighted to have been asked by Robert to write the foreword to this, his second book. But I think it's the least he can do after I gave him the original idea to do his first! I still haven't received any kind of royalty cheque either. But hey, why should that stop me from doing this?

Joking apart, I felt both very pleased, and somewhat proud, at the success of Banksy's first book, *An Irrational Hatred of Luton*, and expect this follow up to be just as well received. It's the nature of the beast, a human trait, well, mine if you like, that when one of your own is successful, in whatever field they are in, you get a great sense of fulfilment yourself from their success. Well, that's how it was for me when *Irrational* was so highly acclaimed. And I'd be telling little white ones if I didn't admit to being as pleased as punch to feature so prominently myself first time around.

I think *Irrational* broke the mould in football books. It was a funny and realistic account of life following West Ham United. But you didn't need to be a West Ham fan to understand it. It was there for everyone. This book follows on from where the last finished. And Robert continues the story in his own unique style.

Many good things have developed since the start of my fanzine, *Over Land and Sea*, and a few of the writers have gone on to join the massed ranks of British journalism. Banksy hasn't but after reading his first book, and by the time you get to the end of this one, you will find it hard to understand why not. People who can write candidly, honestly, and, well, people who can transfer a sense of humour to paper – they are the kind of writers who people want to read. Banksy is one of them. You are going to love this book as much as he obviously enjoyed writing it, and as much as I have enjoyed some of the events you will now read about.

Folkestone, Kent,
September 2000

CONTENTS

INTRODUCTION

On October 19, 1995, *An Irrational Hatred of Luton* was published. Since that day I have had many people approach me asking when the next instalment will be available, and until recently I always replied it would take at least another 10 years to build up the wealth of experience needed to draw on to write another volume.

Yet, a mere five years on from the completion of the original manuscript, the sequel is already down on paper. The more cynical among you might say I have done this for the money. Those of you who know me better will know the reason is more therapeutic – to stop me going nuts and also, because we have experienced enough in the last five years to more than compare with the 20 preceding them.

Not only that, it's always healthy to embarrass friends.

In recent seasons, West Ham United have been viewed as a major force in the Premiership, in particular following the signing of John Hartson and Paul Kitson in February 1997. They scored the goals that saved us from relegation that season and propelled us to the heady heights of eighth place in the table, at the time our best finish for 12 long, hard years.

The following season, we forked out a small fortune for players prepared to make the journey to a seemingly ambitious and potentially successful West Ham; yet now we are almost back at square one. West Ham have always been a laughing stock for the rest of the league, not big enough to be considered major players, nor small enough to be given the benevolent sympathy bestowed on the likes of Charlton Athletic, Ipswich Town or Bradford City.

This book is the story of our Premiership journey through my eyes, the person I consider to be just a fan who, through circumstances not totally within my own control, has come closer to the club than many would dream of.

Irrational was a huge success as far as I was concerned. Goal after goal was achieved in a remarkably short space of time. After actually managing to get the book published in the first place, it quickly went into second edition, something else I never dared hope for. The second edition also sold out and the publishers and myself decided to quit while we were ahead. The book received a decent amount of artistic praise. That, along with the many letters I received from all over the world, expressing empathy for my situation, and telling me what the book had meant to them (and asking when the sequel was due), has given me more pleasure than any of the few measly coppers I raked in as a result. That's not a dig at my publisher, by the way

Irrational finished with a brief synopsis of the 1994-95 season. This book starts with a more considered reflection and finishes at the end of a somewhat eventful 1999-2000 campaign. I hope this account will give you a fan's eye view of the last few years of the century, and prepare you for what can only be more of the same in the new millennium. Now an established and successful Premiership side, I also hope this book will remind you what it was like to support a team that couldn't string two passes together, let alone two league wins. May it also serve as a warning to anyone who might think of supporting West Ham because they are a successful side. What goes around comes around. And what goes up, must come down.

I have tried to make this volume stand alone, without

the need for you to have read the first book. I hope it makes as much sense to you as it does to me.

Robert Banks, October 2000

1. Love Is All Around

Liverpool 0 West Ham United 0 10.9.94

No. Let me start again. Let me go back to the beginning and change things. Let me go back to May 1975 and beg my father to let me go to the park with my friends instead of sitting indoors to watch the FA Cup final. Let it not be the first thing I saw on our shiny brand new colour TV, let it not be the start of a hopeless addiction, to which I am only just starting to find the cure.

Let things be different.

No chance. I have to ask myself, if I did have that chance, the opportunity to rewind my life and do things differently, whether I would take it? Given the chance, I could have opted at the time for a less than successful Manchester United – and be covering myself in glory now. I could be writing books about the treble, about Sir Alex Ferguson's genius and wit (if there is enough for a pamphlet, I would be surprised), or what it's like to be called a wanker every time you pull on a red shirt.

Fortunately, I made the right choice. Becoming a West Ham United supporter was the best decision I ever made and, like most of the best decisions you ever make, they are sub-conscious. Like the decision not to cross the road when there is an Eddie Stobart lorry coming, supporting West Ham, for me, just seemed, well, natural.

And natural it stayed, as natural as the act of breathing, and if you have read *Irrational* you will know all about that. Things were changing, however. Sky Television had taken over and "The Premiership" was now the ultimate goal. The old First Division had been an old fashioned competition, right enough, and the standard had, at times, been pathetic. Something had been needed for some time to pep things up, to bring a bit more professionalism, more exciting players and bigger gates back to an English game still suffering the after-effects of Hillsborough, Heysel, and frankly awful international campaigns.

Now, it seemed choices had to be made. The children running along Green Street no longer unquestioningly supported the Hammers. They wore Arsenal shirts. They wore Tottenham shirts. And, even more worrying, they wore Manchester United shirts. The days when kids could get on to the North Bank and watch a game for 50p were long gone. Football was now everywhere, it was easy to support any team you wanted, and watch most of their matches on TV, without having to come from that geographical area (much to the relief of Manchester United and Liverpool).

Fortunately, I didn't have to make the choice. I was already a Hammers fan and had been for 20 years. The changes occurring in the game, however, meant that watching football would never be the same again. Certainly not for this average Joe.

When I wrote *An Irrational Hatred of Luton* my memories were of a simple game played and enjoyed by simple folk. The game has changed so much that rule no longer applies. Football is big, massive, huge business. So huge that the likes of you and me, who used to enjoy the game for its obvious pleasures, have now, to a greater or lesser extent, been marginalised.

That must be taken into account when reading the pages that follow. What follows is an account of the modern game, through the eyes of an old stick in the mud. It may sound like I am knocking the status quo. Far from it. I am delighted to see West Ham back where they belong. But there has been a high price to pay.

So where did I leave you? Ah yes, 1994. Funny old year. A nutcase flew his plane into the White House and the Queen visited Russia. Both reasonably un-interesting and ultimately pointless exercises. For the first time in my life I found myself unemployed, facing a change of career, no money, no prospects and no regular girlfriend. My love of football kept me going. I have often described football as a religion, and I stand by that belief. We all have things that give us strength in moments of weakness. When I am feeling low, I put on an old West Ham video, read a back issue of a fanzine, or stroll to the pub in my Hammers shirt, and I immediately feel uplifted. It is a curious anomaly of the human male but one I am not inclined to argue with. Other folk require much more complex remedies.

I had been offered some hope from The Wonderful Helen that things might change. Her boyfriend, my best mate at the time, had split with her because he had become convinced we were having an affair. She described this as "quite preposterous". I laughed in agreement, then sadly realised she wasn't joking.

On the job front, I would spend my mornings in September 1994 sending off my CV to uninterested parties. My afternoons and evenings ensconced in front of the glimmering word processor, tapping out my life in 1,500 word segments, never knowing if the rest of the world would ever get to share them. But, as my literary hero T.S. Garp always said: "A writer writes." It was boring. God, it was boring. But there was enough football around at the time to take my mind off things. And a pub at the foot of my stairs with a sympathetic landlord, allowing me to watch all Sky TV games nursing just one pint of lager through the evening.

I still managed to make plenty of games, though. Irons club membership, with its concessions for the unemployed, meant that tickets were still affordable. My involvement with the fanzine, *Over Land and Sea*, also meant that I often got into press boxes on away trips, negating the need for a ticket in the first place, which was nice.

After a rain-soaked defeat at the hands of a rampant Newcastle United, West Ham gathered an unlikely point at a building site known as Anfield. To say Anfield is not the happiest of hunting grounds for the Hammers is like saying Gazza is a bit of a prat. Nevertheless, a 0-0 draw doubled our points tally for the season, on a day when Tony Cottee returned to the fold – and promptly got himself sent off.

This was mildly remarkable. TC sent off! The very fact he had made a challenge in the first place raised a few eyebrows. Add to that he had gone in all guns blazing on Rob Jones, missed the ball completely and made a challenge Vinny Jones would have been proud of in his prime, was nothing short of unbelievable.

TC was welcome back, though. How we had missed someone with his predatory instincts. Lee Chapman had dug us out of a hole the year before but it was clear this wasn't going to be enough to keep our heads above water this term. Despite finishing top scorer in six of his seven seasons at Everton, TC is still not given the credit he deserves on murkeyside. His return to Upton Park gave the side a well needed boost. In the following game, at home to Aston Villa, I filled out my betting slip carefully, putting Cottee down as first goalscorer. My nephew, Mark, not as confident as me, put his pound on 0-0. With five minutes to go it looked like Mark would be collecting, until TC stole into the box and lashed in a Tim Breacker cross in a fashion that brought tears of happy nostalgia to the eyes. Maybe we would be okay after all.

2. Saturday Night

Walsall 2 West Ham United 1 20.9.94

My first major away trip of the season came at Walsall. The day out began on a sour note. Stuart, the QPR fan, telephoned me to tell me his marriage to Vicky was over; he had left and was living back at home with his parents. Shocked? Yes I was. If ever there appeared to be a perfect marriage on the face of things, there it was. Just goes to show how wrong you can be.

Gary rang and asked me to join the OLAS crew on their trip. I had been with them to Exeter a few weeks earlier, for Eamonn Dolan's testimonial, and had a great time, so I jumped at the opportunity. I was without a car, now being unemployed and having run a company car for four years. It came as a shock to be without wheels, relying on British Rail and London Transport. Nasty. I arrived at Redbridge station and met "Clicker" Jason, the OLAS photographer, driver for the day, and sellers John and James. We picked Gary up and immediately found he was in a silly mood. He came out to the car carrying a huge bag of sweets, including a large number of the fabled Little Chef Lollies, much prized among OLAS writers.

We arrived at Bescot stadium at about 4pm. With kick-off not due until 7.45 we had some serious time to kill. Gary told Jason to stop at the local supermarket and returned with a large sack-full of cheap footballs. There were loads of them, possibly enough to keep Wimbledon going for an entire first half. The problem arose when we tried to fit five people and 12 footballs into a Ford Escort with an already full boot. When the car door opened we all flew out like champagne corks.

We started our friendly kickabout, finding that ball control wasn't top of our list of capabilities, but then we were playing with balls lighter than Don Hutchison's head, so it was no real surprise. The highlight of the game was watching John attempt to retrieve the ball from a puddle with an almighty swipe of his left peg, missing it completely and showering Gary with muddy water.

By 6pm, most of us had had enough and wanted food. All except Gary, who had been bragging all day that he'd consumed 10 fish fingers, chips and peas for breakfast. His breath, not to mention other bodily emissions, certainly confirmed this and we did not encourage him to join us. No sooner had we set up stall to start selling the fanzine, than the heavens opened. I took the opportunity to wimp out of selling and collect our press passes, taking my seat in the stand to avoid the rain.

The match was a big non-event. As most of you will no doubt recall, we lost 2-1, with Steve Potts scoring *their* winner, after they had equalised on *our* behalf. The bizarre 90 minutes was followed by an equally bizarre episode in the players' bar, where the five of us had sneaked in unnoticed and were quietly sipping beers until midnight.

Alvin Martin had won the West Ham man-of-the-match award and was reluctantly dragged up from the dressing room to receive his bottle of cheap champagne. As he left, Gary suggested to him that after the performance given by the team that night, Harry Redknapp might not be too impressed seeing him get on the coach carrying a bottle of champagne. "Eh, yer right there, whack" said Alvin, who promptly donated the bottle to our homeward bound fund. The match sponsors were spitting fire. They had gone to all the trouble of going to the supermarket to buy this £2.99 bottle of Asti, and the ungrateful winner promptly gives it away to some oik with tattoos and four of his rough looking mates, who hadn't been invited in the first place. It was a tremendous feeling.

A combination of events, which included leaving Walsall well past midnight and having to catch the night bus home from Trafalgar Square, meant that I didn't get in until about a quarter-to-five the following morning. The feel good factor didn't last, though. The following Sunday we lost 2-0 at home to Arsenal, with Cottee suspended. Chapman and Marsh looked about as likely to score as eunuchs in the desert.

The next Saturday I prepared for the trip to Stamford Bridge by going to a party at a friend's house and getting seriously drunk. Who should be there but Jenny, an ex-girlfriend I hadn't seen for ages. We sat in the corner and talked. Things had never been properly explained why I had let our relationship slide away, why she had never questioned my decisions, why we hadn't talked since. Bottom line was we didn't know, so we ended up snogging in the corner again, setting more than just our own tongues wagging. I was happy, or so I thought. If we could just score a goal at Chelsea tomorrow, that would make my weekend.

3. Baby Come Back

Chelsea 1 West Ham United 2 2.10.94

Jenny was on my mind as I travelled to Stamford Bridge on the train. I had suddenly remembered why we had split up the first time. She bored me senseless. That might sound a little harsh, coming from a man who professes not to be the most exciting in the world, but it was a fact. One I might have remembered sooner had I not consumed more than my fair share of sherbet the night before.

Still, there was a game to be getting on with, and get on with it I did. Glenn Hoddle's Chelsea side had started well with four wins from their opening six games and, on paper, should have murdered us. But that's the beauty of this game. We made them look silly, on their own patch. It was beautiful. Martin Allen started the scoring after the much-maligned 'Chappy' had won a corner, and a Chelsea player provided the perfect flick-on for 'Mad Dog' to bury the opening goal.

A mistake from Ludo Miklosko allowed Furlong to equalise but it was to be West Ham's day. John Moncur cut in from the left to score the winner. And just to add the cherry on the top of the cake, Steve Clarke was sent off for a dreadful challenge on Allen. After beating Chelsea and Villa, and getting a draw at Anfield, maybe our optimism was not as badly misplaced as we had first thought. With four teams facing the drop from a league of 22, it would mean that a serious number of points would be required to make Premiership status safe, but we were well on the way. Walsall were safely tucked away in the second leg of the Coca-Cola cup-tie, albeit after extra time, with goals from Moncur and Hutchison. 'Moncs' had now scored two in two games and was looking like the great attacking midfield player we had been missing since the departure of, er, Martin Peters. Wrong!

As wrong as I had been to get together with Jenny again. That Friday night I cooked dinner for her and she explained to her parents she would be spending the night with me at my flat, only for me to break the news to her over dinner that I had made a big mistake, and was really sorry. I must have been mad. There was a definite shag on there.. But I'm not that sort of bloke. I couldn't have told her in the morning. Couldn't have lived with myself. As it turned out, I was the only person I could live with.

Billed as a relegation six-pointer so early in the season, the home match against Crystal Palace took on extra significance. With Cottee still missing, we won a tight game 1-0 with another goal from 'Deadly' Don Hutchison. The win heralded a barren spell – not just for me, but for West Ham United. Sure, the conquering hero was to return to the club that had made him. Sure, we would win matches against Southampton and Leicester City and delight in another triumph against Chelsea. But it would also see us lose six out of eight of the next league matches, and get knocked out of the Coca-Cola Cup playing, arguably, some of the worst football ever witnessed at Upton Park. Two matches in particular had to be seen to be believed.

4. Let Me Be Your Fantasy

West Ham United 2 Southampton 0   22.10.94

It was fate. No sooner had I pressed the final key in completing the manuscript of the first draft of *Irrational*, than the telephone rang and I was offered a job. Nothing very exciting, a valuation officer at Lambeth Valuation Office, settling council tax appeals for the merry burgers of Streatham.

Celebrating this news, I went off to France with some friends rather than face the prospect of the trip to Old Trafford, where Manchester United halted our progress with a 1-0 win. Cantona scored after a mistake from good old Alvin, who lost the flight of the ball in the air in a manner which suggested he had kept that bottle of champagne after all. While the majority of the Hammers faithful who had made the trip returned to London empty handed, I at least had a few dozen bottles of cheap plonk plus some dodgy cheese with walnuts in it.

The news that followed brought a broad grin to everyone's face. Julian Dicks had re-signed for West Ham. It had been on the cards for some time because Dicksy was clearly out of favour at Liverpool. Gary once asked Roy Evans, the Liverpool manager at the time, off the record, how much he would sell Julian for. Evans replied: "How much have you got on you?" The writing was on the wall from that moment.

There was really only one club Julian could have gone to. With a leg that was likely to go off bang at any minute, just like his temper, he was a risk that most

Premiership managers would not have taken. Yet we got him back for a song, a figure rumoured to be around the £350,000 mark, significantly lower than the fee we had sold him for.

Jules made his second debut for West Ham in the home game against Southampton. I sat in the West Lower, eagerly awaiting the return of the hero. Now shaven-headed, Jules displayed the same tigerish attitude we had grown to love during his first spell as West Ham strolled to a 2-0 win. Allen and Matthew Rush scored the second half goals that secured the points, and with Cottee and a booked Dicks back in the fold, the West Ham faithful could have been forgiven for thinking the best was yet to come.

A narrow victory at home to Chelsea in the Coke Cup followed, Hutchison scoring the only goal in the second minute from the edge of the box. We were fortunate to hang on for a victory for the remaining 88 minutes.

Unfortunately a lot worse was yet to come. A bad tempered game at White Hart Lane (on and off the pitch) ended in a 3-1 victory for the Tott Scum and turned out to be Ossie Ardiles' swansong. Unbelievably, Everton hadn't won a game by the time we visited Goodison Park on November 1. Form suggested they would still be looking on November 2 but this is West Ham. Everton grabbed a 1-0 win with a goal from their ace striker Gary Ablett.

Work at the valuation office proved to be incredibly dull. I worked flexi-time, which meant I could start and finish when I liked, as long as I was there between 10am and 4pm. Work was very slack, though, and I would often find myself sloping off to Waterloo station at 4.05pm. After all, there are only so many times you can go to the toilet. Pretending to look busy is a lot harder than actually *being* busy.

There wasn't really a good camaraderie there. Most of

the people were on temporary contracts, and those who had been there longer than six months were quite cliquey. But it was a job, and I was grateful for that. I arrived home one evening to be followed up the stairs by my insurance man, who had a cheque for me. I had been saving £5 a month in an endowment policy and it had come to fruition. I fully expected him to try and flog me another one. I wasn't disappointed. He arranged to come back and see me the following evening, with his manager, and we ended up talking about everything except savings.

Basically, they felt I would be a prime candidate for a job they had going, that of Co-Operative Insurance Society (CIS) agent. I was dubious but made an appointment to go along for an interview. It had to be better than staring at a computer screen all day.

Meanwhile West Ham managed a 1-0 victory over Leicester City at Upton Park. Moncur was hacked down in the area and Dicksy dispatched his first penalty since his return. Hutchison had been sent off earlier in the game for two horrendous tackles. His Upton Park career was in jeopardy from that point on. In Harry's view, Hutch had put the welfare of the team at risk with his recklessness. He was our record signing, however, so he had to be played at every opportunity.

The next game was away at Hillsborough. Gary, me and John, the seller, were joined by a spotty youth by the name of Scott as we hired a car from Stanstead airport. I had the honour of driving my first OLAS away trip, collecting no less than 110 Little Chef lollies en route. We pissed on Sheffield Wednesday from a great height. We lost 1-0. Rushie appeared to have the freedom of the Hillsborough pitch but couldn't find a colleague with any of his aimless crosses. Dan Petrescu scored their winner and the trip home was illuminated only by the fact that two of us won £10 on the first ever

National Lottery draw, plus the fact that we gave Scott a hard time.

"What's yer mum like?" Gary would ask him. Scotty would go bright red and say: "Er, well, about 40, five foot six, brown hair..."

"Noooo, what's your mum like?" Gary sniggered. "Elton John? The Beatles? What?"

"Oh yeah, Elton John and Phil Collins."

"No, I mean what's she like?"

Well, you get the idea. It helped to pass the time.

The next league game came at Upton Park against Coventry City. Despite our recent run of results, this was Coventry City, so we always felt confident of getting a result. What followed was possibly the worst 90 minutes of football I have ever experienced as a Hammers fan. Not only did the team lack penetration, they seemed unable to pass the ball with any accuracy or conviction. All the players looked lazy and disinterested. I've seen us take heavier beatings than this but never before had I seen a home performance that left me feeling the team just didn't care. The fact Coventry were only marginally better contributed to the dross, and they won by a scrappy goal scored by David Buust.

It had been a while since I had felt so low as a West Ham supporter. After all, we had spent big money (by our standards) and lured back former heroes, yet it seemed we still could not even compete with the Coventry Citys and Sheffield Wednesdays of this world.

We had the chance to redeem ourselves in the Coca-Cola Cup. Just our luck, though, to have to play a buoyant Bolton Wanderers side who were not only riding high in the First Division, but who had also recently disposed of Liverpool, Everton, Arsenal and Aston Villa in cup competitions.

I remember watching the draw on TV. At the time they had it on breakfast television, at some unearthly hour.

Ray Wilkins had been drafted in to provide 'expert' analysis of the draw.

"Well, Ralph," Ray crooned, "some exceptional ties there, tremendous." I cringed, continuing to iron my shirt with one hand and eat my breakfast with the other. "Blackburn against Liverpool, what an exceptional prospect that is, both playing super football at the moment and this promises to be a lovely game of football" I considered applying for his job, or just hiring a hit-man. "And then of course there's Manchester City against Newcastle, super, quite remarkable."

After looking at every tie, Wilkins could see he'd missed one. "Oh, and West Ham against Bolton, which is of course a repeat of the 1923 Cup final, super, exceptional." I wondered about the relevance of the game being a repeat of the 1923 FA Cup final. Was this a bad omen? After all, Bolton had won that game 2-0. On the other hand, I reasoned, it was also a repeat of the 1967 third round tie, which West Ham won 4-1, so we were on a level playing field. I checked the records and found that we had also won a second round game 7-2 in 1968, so felt a lot happier about the tie.

One of the few social events to take place at Lambeth Valuation Office occurred the same day, as one of the girls was leaving and we trooped down to Pizza Hut for an all-you-can-eat buffet. It was a measure of the way I felt about my colleagues, and no doubt the way they felt about me, that I couldn't wait to get back to the office and read the paper in the toilet.

Unfortunately, the game, which promised much, failed to deliver, and West Ham were beaten easily 3-1. At least we showed a modicum of determination and fight but only after we found ourselves three down. Cottee scored his first goal for nine matches, an appalling record symptomatic of a team playing some pathetic football. The prize of a place in the quarter-finals had been snatched away by a Bolton side destined to lose in the final to Liverpool, and win promotion at the end of the season. The low would continue, Redknapp's position was called into question. Sitting in 17th position in a League of 22 with four to go down, relegation looked a very real possibility. However, Hammers fans are an optimistic bunch. If George Foreman could regain his world heavyweight title as a grandfather at the age of 45, then surely Redknapp could guide the Hammers out of their current plight?

5. Stay Another Day

Leeds United 2 West Ham United 2 10.12.94

The slide had to be arrested somehow. Harry, frustrated by lack of funds, knew he had to bring in some fresh blood to boost morale as well as results. Hampered by lack of transfer funds, he brought in Northern Ireland international Michael Hughes on loan from French club Strasbourg. I had been a fan of Hughes' since his days at Manchester City and hadn't really understood why they had let him go in the first place. Now I didn't care, I was delighted to see him as a West Ham player.

December began with a trip across London to Shepherds Bush to face QPR in a live Sunday afternoon Sky game. I watched the match with Stuart, the QPR fan, and his father, Dave, in the Ellerslie Road stand, trying very hard to hide my disappointment as first Les Ferdinand rose above the defence unchallenged to make it 1-0, then Trevor Sinclair doubled QPR's lead with a good strike after a mazy but ultimately free run. At 2-0, though, West Ham started playing. Hughes looked to be as good a player as he'd been at Man. City and once he had found his feet, West Ham started to tick. Cottee's deep cross found the head of Jeroen Boere and the deficit was halved. Alas, too late again, and a sixth defeat from seven games was the outcome.

At least defeat had not been so inevitable. Even at 2-0 to QPR, the outcome of the game was in question until the end and we detected a hint of a revival. But with the next match away at Elland Road, it seemed we might have to wait for that revival to bear any fruit. Gary and I travelled to Leeds alone, a rarity for an OLAS trip. With it being the last away jaunt before Christmas, and the majority crying off through holiday and female commitments, we bombed up the M1 more in hope than expectation.

As we flew over the crest of the M62, we felt we were entering another world, a world of back-to-back terraced houses, cloth caps, warm beer and whippets. But that might be construed as a little stereotypical, so I won't say that here.

We arrived in very good time, three-and-a-half hours early in fact, parking in a car park that resembled a World War One battlefield. Gary got a call from our friends in the north, Liam and Sean Tyrrell, Wakefield lubbers now but born in Romford and still devoted Hammers.

Liam warned us to be on the lookout for trouble, as some West Ham fans had been up the night before causing grief in the city centre. Gary and I both found that very hard to believe (honest) but I took the precaution of hiding my jacket so as not to appear too obvious. Gary called the Jacket my "shit" jacket, not just for its appearance, but because it had "Pony" emblazoned across the back. I think he was jealous.

Being so early, we took the opportunity to have a wander around the stadium. It was the first time I had seen the new 17,000 capacity stand and it was mightily impressive, even if it did remind me a little of East Croydon railway station. As we walked around the ground, past the banqueting halls and the press areas, it struck me what a big club Leeds United is. Having been to Sheffield Wednesday, another big club, a few weeks before, it struck me that Leeds had a lot more style and professionalism in their approach to fleecing people for money.

They also employ some real jailbait on matchdays. This occurred to me as I stood outside waiting for Gary to collect his press pass, and I almost wore out my smile. Very nice.

We got down to the real business of selling the fanzine after chatting to all the regulars. We expected the usual rush of abuse we get at about 2.50pm but all I got was a pissed Leeds fan muttering "wanker" under his breath as he sped past at 80 mph. Very brave. Gary was pre-empting any potentially explosive situations by shouting: "Yes, I do know who my dad is and no, I'm not a cockney!"

A young female West Ham fan approached me and asked me where the "other fat fanzine seller" was. Without thinking, I pointed at Gary. But as she left, I thought, hang on a minute, what does she mean *other* fat fanzine seller! Bloody cheek.

Before Gary and I had made it to our seats we were a goal down, and a second followed soon afterwards. It seemed the traditional Elland Road spanking was on the cards. But just before half-time, Keith Rowland swung in a high cross and Boere got his nut on it to make it 2-1 at half time. The West Ham fans went berserk. Not only a goal, but a goal away from home. Not only a goal away from home, but a goal at Elland Road. Not only a goal at Elland Road, but a goal from a cross by Keith Rowland. I could go on...

In the second half, the unthinkable happened, as West Ham outplayed their hosts and Boere grabbed a deserved equaliser. Now we went potty. Boere ran to our corner to celebrate as the mouthy Leeds fans behind the goal started to file out. I couldn't decide which was the more satisfying sight.

As Gary and I trooped off to the press conference, I couldn't hide my satisfaction as I pointed out I had called for Boere to be in the team several months ago. Gary muttered something about me being a self-righteous bastard, a bit of a Frank Doberman, so I went into character and said: "That Jeroen Boere is welcome to come and have tea and biscuits with me and the wife any time he likes. But if he starts jumping up and down and spouting Dutch nonsense about the Maastricht Treaty and demanding a first team place in my kitchen, I'd have to say: Oi! Boere, No! I admire the way you ghost in at the far post a la Martin Peters, and your English is almost perfect, but I will not allow this behaviour in my place of abode!" You had to be there really.

The press conference was fun. Gary asked Harry Redknapp if he was disappointed we hadn't won the game. Harry said he'd have been more than happy with a point at 2-0 down. I could see what Gary was driving at, though, expressing my view that Boere should have been in the team a lot earlier in the campaign. While waiting for Leeds manager Howard Wilkinson to come in, we were cornered by some local hacks asking us questions about Boere. It was quite sad really. Wilkinson arrived and silence fell. He scares the shit out of me and no doubt a lot of the other more experienced journos, too. He's like the strict teacher no one messed with. Needless to say he wasn't a happy man. But then it's hard to tell with him.

Gary drove us home while we scoffed lemon bon-bons and a big bag of Revels, shouting along to *All Around the World* by *The Jam*. We talked, as we did on most away trips, about what we would do if we won the lottery. As we spoke, we passed the Charlton Athletic team coach,and I could see Mark Robson sitting in the back looking totally miserable. Some of my winnings would have to go on bringing him back to Upton Park. But not this week. Not even a sodding tenner this week.

I stopped off for a chow mein on the way home and noticed that 1994 was the Chinese Year of the Dog. 1995 was to be the Year of the Boar. Or should that be the year of the Boere?

6. Love Me For A Reason

Blackburn Rovers 4 West Ham United 2 2.1.95

My career, such as it was, was taking a few twists and turns. The work at the valuation office wasn't particularly taxing, neither was it stimulating. On the other hand, it was good money for reasonable hours and I was largely left to my own devices. We played football once a week and I could have been in much worse places. However, I knew my contract was to run out at the end of March, so I was looking around for another job, knowing the chances of an extended contract at the VO were slim.

The chance came from the CIS. I'd had an interview with the district office manager, Chris, who had visited me at home to check me out. It seemed that I was in line for the job, I just had to wait for the nod. Knowing there was a job on the horizon made me feel a lot more comfortable as I headed into Christmas 1994. My social life had suffered because I had no car and couldn't really be bothered to get the bus anywhere, so football provided me with my only recreation, other than a swift pint at the Elmer Lodge, or a visit from Mark, an old mate from way back, who had come back on the scene after a lengthy gap. He didn't mind driving over to me, so we would often nip over the pub for a swift half and put the world to rights.

The last match before Christmas was the home game against Manchester City. I'd been looking forward to it for three reasons: Firstly, the encounter with City the previous season had been a classic, with West Ham winning 3-1. This game promised more of the same. Secondly, West Ham's improving form meant I was looking forward to games, not dreading them. And thirdly, it was the OLAS writers' Christmas party afterwards.

I sat in the West Lower and watched a brilliant individual display from Cottee (about time) as he poached one with each foot in the first half, then capped a good dribble with a powerful shot to complete his hat-trick in the second half. A 3-0 victory was a great result to take into Christmas and gave us revenge for the similar scoreline we had suffered at Maine Road in August.

I left the OLAS bash early to go to a party in Orpington, thinking I had a chance with a young lady by the name of Emily. Should have stayed with the OLAS boys. You knew where you stood with them.

After a fairly tepid Christmas, Boxing Day brought a home match against struggling Ipswich Town. This was the only home game of the season I missed, as I was in Hastings for a family gathering. I did see some football, though. I went to see local side Stamco (now known as Stamcroft St Leonards) beat Margate 3-0. I made regular trips to the bar to watch Ceefax and see if we had held on to Cottee's opener but, West Ham being West Ham, they allowed Claus Thomsen to equalise and couldn't improve on a 1-1 draw. A couple of days later came a trip to Selhurst Park and a display almost as tepid as my Christmas against a very ordinary Wimbledon side. The game finished 1-0 to the Dons. West Ham were a little unlucky not to get a point but they didn't stick their chances away. That was put right on New Year's Eve against a Nottingham Forest side riding high in the Premiership following promotion, and on course for a place in Europe.

In pouring rain, I sat in the lower tier of the almost

completed Centenary Stand and watched with nephew Mark as we raced into a 3-0 first half lead, playing some delightful football. Cottee grabbed his fifth in four games, Ian Bishop knocked in a near post corner and Hughes grabbed his first for the club. The "dangerous" Stanley Collymore had been kept very quiet by a certain Alvin Martin, almost old enough to be his dad and enjoying the twilight of his career. At a time when most were losing their head, it was good to have Alvin around to calm things down and play the ball out from the back.

The game finished 3-1 and 1994, a somewhat turbulent year for me personally, at least ended on a high from a football point of view. I held a New Year's Eve party at my flat and was worried at one point that the floor was going to collapse. Even the folks downstairs joined in the fun by banging merrily on the ceiling at two in the morning.

The fixture computer had at least been kind enough to give me a day off on New Year's Day, enough time to recover before the trip to Blackburn on the Bank Holiday Monday. Phil Daniels, OLAS writer extraordinaire (believe me, extraordinary is the best way to describe Phil) was driving, with just Gary and me as company. A trip to Blackburn was not high on my wish list on that particular day. With sub-zero temperatures in London I had to force myself reluctantly out of my warm bed to make the rendezvous point of Redbridge station, which resembled an ice rink.

We headed off, with lumps of ice and snow falling off the car, not stopping until we reached a service station well up the M6. I had washed my hair that morning and couldn't do a thing with it. My woolly hat had not helped matters and by the time we reached Knutsford it was looking decidedly dodgy. Phil christened me "Woody Woodpecker", which I thought was a bit rich coming from a bloke who's principal nickname is "Baldy."

We parked in a pub car park, marshalled by an unfortunate youth with a complexion like a bucket of maggots. It was still freezing but not as cold as it had felt in London. Phil and Gary nipped round the back of the pub for a slash just as a uniformed WPC pulled up in a car in front of them. She got out of the car with a broad grin on her face, so we weren't sure if she just saw the humour of the situation, or she'd caught a glimpse of Phil's dick. Well, it was *very* cold. We set up stall outside Ewood Park. Phil was shouting louder than anyone: "Come and get your OLAS, as written in by Woody Woodpecker". Cheeky git. I'd had enough of the cold, so went for a beer with Liam and Sean before taking my seat to witness a truly memorable game.

Blackburn Rovers were the millionaire outfit, cruising their way to the Premiership title. West Ham were the rag and bone men from down the street, yet it looked for a long time like we could spoil the party. An outrageous dive from Shearer brought them the penalty that put them 1-0 up. But then West Ham took over and a brilliant display from Matty Holmes set up a fightback. Cottee equalised just before half-time, then from a corner, Dicks put us 2-1 ahead, to the delight of the travelling fans. We were playing so well, we sensed that it could even last. But this was Blackburn Rovers, this was to be their year, and they were going to have the last say.

A freekick from Graeme Le Saux trickled under Tim Breacker's foot on the line to make it 2-2 and two more from Shearer, including another dodgy penalty, made the final score 4-2. It left Blackburn mightily relieved but West Ham the moral victors.

Gary and Phil had press passes, so I had arranged to meet them outside the main gates after the game. After almost an hour they still had not emerged, so I approached the uniformed girl on the door and asked her permission to go through. Reluctant at first, I told her I was press but didn't have a pass, and merely wanted to meet some colleagues. She took pity on me and after a little chat we went on a guided tour of the main stand. She showed me the press room, which resembled a cinema, but it was empty. "Where's the press conference?" I asked. "Oh, that'll be in't tunnel," she replied. I was amused that with all these cosy facilities available on a freezing cold day in January, they still chose to hold the press conference on the pitch.

I wandered down unattended, nodding to Ludo (the goalkeeper, not my cat) as he left the dressing room, then pinching myself, reminding myself that this was real. I passed Ray Harford doing an interview for *Match of the Day* in the tunnel, as Alan Shearer headed towards me, match ball under his arm. The little boy in me got the better of me. I had to do it. No, I didn't call him a lucky tosser. I asked him to sign my programme.

Out on the pitch I found the reason for the delay. Gary and Phil had bumped into former Upton Park favourite Tony Gale and were having a chinwag with him. Dumped on by West Ham, it was nice to see "Reggie" doing well at Blackburn. Although we didn't know for certain at the time, he was soon to collect a Championship winner's medal.

We returned to the car to find the car park empty. What should have been an easy drive back proved to be anything but as we detoured via Blackpool, due in part to heavy traffic on the M6 but also to some very suspect navigation. I missed the last train to Beckenham and had to get one to Croydon instead. The buses had all finished and I had no dosh left for a cab, so I walked home from Croydon, listening to Darren Gough destroying the Australians on my Walkman. That proved to be a false dawn. Would 1995 be a false dawn for me, or for West Ham United?

7. Cotton Eye Joe

West Ham United 1 Tottenham Hotspur 2 14.1.95

The FA Cup offered us a little crumb of comfort; a respite from the hurly-burly of the Premiership. As with Bolton Wanderers in the Coca-Cola, though, we drew a high-flying lower division team in the third round, in the shape of Martin O'Neill's Wycombe Wanderers.

No sooner had the draw been made, than we were tipped to get beaten. The potential upset of the round. Looking back on it now, it was quite a correct assumption to make if you looked at the facts. West Ham, forever brittle against lower division sides in the cup, already knocked out of one competition by Bolton, and knocked out of both cups last season by lower division teams. Wycombe, doing well in the league under a bright young manager, with league titles and European cups to his name, and a good record at home. It all added up to a potential disaster.

I suppose that's what makes football the game it is. Never knowing what's going to happen next. Although we condemned Alan Hansen and others for making such predictions, deep down we knew they were right. As Gary and I headed for Adams Park, we knew that we were heading for a struggle. Not only that, neither of us had tickets. To distract us, we stopped off on the way into Wycombe as a ladies' hockey match had grabbed our attention. Well, it would have been rude not to stop and have a look, wouldn't it?

We arrived at Adams Park to be met by another

atrocious looking car park attendant. What on earth does it say in the adverts for these people? "Wanted: Scrawny youth with no personality to wave arms around in a football car park. Smallpox complexion an advantage but not essential..." This one was so rough we couldn't even tell what sex it was, but 'it' showed us to a convenient spot (no pun intended) where we unloaded the books, plus some snazzy OLAS hats Gary had ordered, which sold out in seconds.

This, in my view, was the hey-day of the fanzine. At this point OLAS had reached that point where it appeared professional yet still remained devilishly cynical. Other fanzines can go too far in any one direction. Too amateur and they are unreadable, so professional they look, and read, like an official club publication, or so cynical that it's impossible to take anything from it. OLAS, biased as I am, hit the nail squarely on the head every issue, using the smallest possible hammer.

We met Kevin Williamson in the car park. I was worried about him. He looked like death. I later found out he always looks like this but he was particularly bad that day after getting up at the crack of dawn to queue for tickets for the upcoming Southampton match. He might have looked rough that morning but he had something we didn't have – a match ticket.

The BBC vultures were circling, setting up their cameras to feast on the dead carcasses of our team once they had succumbed. More ticketless fans turned up, complaining that the touts at the end of the road were quoting £20-£30 for a terrace ticket with a face value of a fiver.

By two o'clock, however, we were sorted. That's the advantage of being a fanzine seller. Those sensible folk who refuse to deal with touts always offer you a ticket, and if you don't want it they ask you to pass it on at face value. Since I started writing for OLAS I have never missed a game through lack of a ticket. It just takes a bit of patience, effort and trust in the good nature of fellow Hammers.

Those less fortunate perched in trees at the top of the hill and watched West Ham defy the critics, winning the game 2-0. Despite having a nine-foot centre half, Wycombe couldn't stop the two smallest players on the pitch from scoring. Cottee and Kenny Brown got the goals in the white and claret Pony away shirt making its debut in a competitive game.

As the second goal went in, West Ham fans sang loudly *Hansen, Hansen, What's The Score?* So loud was the taunting of the slimy Scottish one, it made a few of the national papers on Sunday. I'd arranged to meet Gary outside but, as usual, he didn't show, so I strode boldly into reception. Gary taught me a lot during this time. If you stride confidently about, looking as though you know where you are going, and you are supposed to be there, then you will rarely be challenged. This was great advice and I used it on this occasion, walking straight into the players' bar, having a chat with Jeroen Boere and Tim Breacker, then buying myself a beer and sitting down to wait for Gary. Hard life.

It was clear that things wouldn't be this good forever. Days like that, in any season, are rare. The call to arms at the CIS came sooner than anticipated and I had to give two days' notice at the valuation office. They were not impressed. Still, this was a permanent job, and one I was looking forward to. My predecessor, Bob Peverett, made a sideways move in the company and was able to show me the ropes. Bob's a great bloke, a really good laugh and we have remained friends to this day. He helped me to settle in, which was important, as this was a complete career change for me. After being involved in property management or valuation my entire career, I had to start again and learn about insurance, finances, pension, endowments, etc. My head was spinning at the thought of all the training but at the same time I was excited by the prospect of a new challenge.

The district office manager, Chris Maflin, being a Tottenham fan, pointed out that we were playing each other the Saturday before I was due to start. I did not need him to draw this to my attention. I was painfully aware of it and also the possibility that I could be in for some serious ribbing on my first day.

The first half of the game produced some of the best football West Ham had played all season. Beautiful flowing moves, one touch, two touch, pass and move, it was a joy to behold. When Boere put us 1-0 up it looked like it would be the first of many. We took extra joy in the knowledge that the goal prevented Ian Walker breaking the Totts' club record for clean sheets.

The first half must have worn them out though. Sloppy second half goals from Klinsmann and Sheringham sent the points back to North London, and me off to work on Monday with my tail between my legs.

At least we didn't lose the following Saturday. Kevin drove us all down to Southampton, only for the heavens to open and the game to be cancelled about an hour before kick-off. Kev was livid. Not only had he driven all the way to Southampton, he couldn't have a beer, the game was off, and he had to put up with our ugly mugs all the way back. A fight in the pub, which ended in one bloke head-butting another, marred the day. After all the fuss had died down, and all aspects of the fight had been fully discussed, young Mark came ambling around the corner with an excited smile on his lips. "Guess what?" he said, "some bloke just got nutted!" It wasn't the first time he'd amused us on away trips and it wouldn't be the last either, poor lad. We had already had some fun at his expense. He had committed the cardinal sin of asking if we could stop for a piss. Knowing he was bursting, we encouraged Kev to keep driving. I arrived home to find Stuart, the QPR fan, had come up with a couple of tickets for the fourth round cup-tie at Loftus Road. Good lad.

Much worse was to follow. Our home game against Sheffield Wednesday was moved to the Monday night by Uncle Rupert, so the ticket I had bought for Lucy couldn't be used, as she was busy. I swapped it for a ticket for the Everton game and sat in the Centenary Upper to witness one of the most bizarre spectacles ever at Upton Park. Alvin Martin was sent off by referee Paul Danson for a tackle on Mark Bright on the halfway line. Sure it was a foul but Alvin had merely stumbled over and Bright had tripped over him. Danson was taking things a little too far.

Waddle scored a terrific goal against our 10 men, before Tim Breacker was also sent off for two bookings. Bright wrapped up a 2-0 win and confidence, such a vital factor in football, was back on the floor again. Not good timing with the cup-tie at QPR just around the corner. All the pundits had sided with Alvin but the fact of the matter was we had lost the game as a result of it, and we were almost back to our form of November.

QPR rubbed salt into the wounds with a 1-0 victory to knock us out of the FA Cup. I took my dad to the game, which turned out to be a huge non-event, with Andrew Impey scoring the winner. There was a diplomatic silence in the car on the way home as we travelled back with Stuart, the QPR fan, and his father Dave. QPR were doing well, in the top half of the league, and had been doing a lot better than West Ham for a number of years. Yet their achievements went largely unrecognised. I suppose it's the unwritten law of football. People would rather talk about Manchester United or Liverpool finishing 10th than about QPR or West Ham finishing fifth. It's a cruel world.

Gary rang me at home very excited. Phil had been at the match between Crystal Palace and Manchester United and witnessed the now infamous Cantona *Kung Fu* kick on Palace fan Matthew Simmons. The debate raged on about whether Simmons had asked for it, or whether Cantona should be banned for a long time. As for West Ham fans, we were just excited at the prospect of Paul Ince getting done for incitement.

8. Think Twice

Leicester City 1 West Ham United 2 4.2.95

The now customary win over Leicester City followed.
The fact we had won at Filbert Street could not hide the
fact that we were crap. After all, we *always* won at Filbert
Street and Leicester were even worse than us. A 2-1
victory came thanks to goals from Cottee and a Dicks
penalty, Mark Robins getting the goal for The Foxes. The
game was remarkable not for the result though, but for
the appearance of City substitute Jamie Lawrence.

We'd enjoyed a brilliant day. Travelling up in two cars,
six of us played football for an hour before the game on
a small, enclosed astroturf pitch near the stadium. The
pitch had been heavily sanded and we played as two
teams of three based on the occupants of the two cars
coming up. The Jeep (me, Gary and the Jughunter) beat
the Sierra (Kev, Scott and Jim Drury) 15-14, but not
before Kev had scared the shit out of me, running out of
his goal screaming "Don't score, you c***!" He went for
the ball, missed it, took my legs away and we both
ended up on our backs in a fit of giggles.

Time came to sell the fanzine but with six of us, we
were fighting for punters like tarts on Streatham
Common. Jim "Morrissey" Drury decided he'd had
enough and started chatting up one of the female
Leicester City stewards. With my impaired vision, from a
distance she didn't look too bad, but closer inspection
revealed she had a moustache Nigel Mansell would
have been proud of.

At 2-1 down, Leicester City manager Mark McGhee gave us all a laugh and put on Jamie Lawrence. Now I know Jamie is a good little player but he had the most ridiculous hair style at the time, his dreadlocks bunched up on top of his head in a kind of pineapple fashion. The West Ham fans there that day could not resist, and I am privileged to say I was present at the birth of one of the funniest football chants ever. To the tune of *He's Got The Whole World In His Hands*, we sang *He's Got A Pineapple On His Head*! It was so infectious and funny that even the Leicester fans started singing along. The song was later pinched by other fans who mainly aimed it at Nottingham Forest's Jason Lee. It affected him so badly, it could have ended his career.

To top the day off nicely, Kev and I sprinted back to his car and were back in his local by 7.30pm. Kev lives in the heart of Arsenal territory and was keen to get back in time to brag about our victory, in full knowledge that Arsenal had lost 3-1 that day and had two players sent off.

Meanwhile, at work I was undergoing intense training, being sent on courses and monitored for this and that. It was hard work but good fun and the pressure to sell wasn't too high because I was still the new boy and not yet qualified. I did sense one problem, though. My round covered a part of the world called Downham. There's not a huge amount of money in Downham and while colleagues were signing up savings policies for £50-£100 per month, I was struggling to get people to commit £10-20

With the job being so new, I wasn't able to get a loan to buy a car. My sister stepped into the breach and took out a loan on my behalf, enabling me to acquire a real dog of a motor in a Ford Orion 1.6i Ghia. I won't go into what exactly was wrong with it, suffice to say the motor is long gone, although the loan is still there.

Everton came to town, heralding the opening of the new Centenary Stand, which replaced the old North Bank. I cannot remember how, but we had some freebies for this game, so I took my dad, my nephew and his mate Luke, who by chance was also the nephew of The Wonderful Helen, whom you may well recall from *Irrational*. Now I was mobile again, I used to go and visit her and try to work my way into her affections. But it wasn't working. Taking her nephew to football couldn't do any harm, though, could it?

The match was played in pouring rain on a Monday evening, once again for the benefit of Sky TV. Cottee scored a fine first half goal to put us in front before Paul Rideout equalised from an impossible angle. Hutch crossed for Cottee to grab a second against his former club but a draw it was destined to be, with Anders Limpar hitting a terrific drive for their second equaliser.

Rain seemed to be a feature of the season. After the abortive trip to Southampton, we had another last minute cancellation for the home match against QPR. Stuart, the QPR fan, had kindly driven me all the way to Upton Park and struggled to find a decent parking spot, only to find on arrival that the game had been called off. Instead we went for a beer in the Black Horse at Lockesbottom, with Sam and Lucy. More enjoyable than West Ham v QPR? Well, maybe.

Kev drove us to Coventry the following Saturday. The rain held off this time but the poor form didn't. Our penchant for playing football before the game manifested itself again, as Jim produced a ball and we went off in search of a suitable venue. There is a park near Highfield Road but after all the rain that had fallen, the ground was a bit soft – so soft, in fact, we had to borrow the park keeper's tractor to pull Jim out after he'd sunk up to his waist. A lady motorist asked for our help, as she'd put her steering lock on and couldn't get it off. After a five-second good Samaritan job, we asked if we could play football in her back garden. She said no. Some people are just so ungrateful. In the end we found a school with a playground, hopped over the gates and played there for an hour or so.

I had a ticket for the match but had also secured a press pass. I offered my ticket to a bloke queuing at the box office. When I said he could have it for nothing, he looked at me like I had three heads.

The match was a pile of shite. West Ham hadn't played well since the first half against the Totts, and Coventry City had the momentum of a new manager in the bulky shape of Big Ron Atkinson. It was obvious what the result was going to be. Not so obvious was that old boy Mike Marsh would set one up and score another in City's 2-0 win.

After the game I bumped into Tony McDonald, Managing Editor of Independent UK Sports Publications, to whom I had submitted a draft of my first book, *An Irrational Hatred of Luton*. To my surprise and delight, he gave me the green light and suggested that I update it and prepare it for publication around October time. Delighted with the news, we took advantage of the free beer on offer in the press box, tried hard to push our way though the hacks interviewing Big Ron. By the time Harry came out there were only five of us, four from OLAS, and one bloke who had turned up late for Big Ron and hadn't wanted to appear rude by leaving.

We didn't really care, we had free beer. It was another world. The steward said he had to go, but showed us how to operate the beer tap. He told us just to shut the door behind us when we left. Kev and I decided to leave shortly after that but I understand the others went down and had a kick-about on the pitch. The groundsman shouted at them and they thought they were going to be told to hop it. Instead, the groundsman pointed at his watch and said: "Five minutes, lads, then I've got to lock up!" I know it was only five years ago but it's hard to see that kind of thing happening anywhere today.

February ended with another defeat. This time at home to Chelsea and, again, from a winning position. Hutch put us 1-0 up but second half goals turned the game around for Chelsea. Cottee appeared to have scored an equaliser late on but the referee ruled it out for a push on the 'keeper by Trevor Morley, but only after the Chelsea players had bullied him into consulting his linesman. Four wins from the last 18 matches was relegation form. Something had to change, and change fast.

9. No More I Love You's

Arsenal 0 West Ham United 1 5.3.95

Things did change. Although the weather didn't. More
rain greeted us at Highbury as we took on Arsenal in a
match we seemed destined to lose. In 20th place in the
Premier League, it didn't take a rocket scientist to work
out we hadn't been playing well. Arsenal, on the other
hand, were playing on the Sunday due to their European
commitments and were heading for their second
successive Cup Winners' Cup final. Who would your
money have been on?

Moncur slipped a clever free-kick through to
Hutchison . . . 1-0 to West Ham, a lead we somehow
held on to. The next day I was sent off to Watford for a
course, so I wasn't able to see us lose 2-0 at Newcastle
United on the Wednesday night. The training officer
taking the course was a Geordie and gave me tons of
stick.

There are defining moments in matches, points where
you can visibly see the tide turn, or a team's heads drop
collectively. I also believe there are defining moments in
a season. That turning point came in the home match
against Norwich City, on March 11. After the win at
Arsenal and an expected defeat at Newcastle,
confidence should have been reasonably high, But West
Ham went 2-0 down again in a match they should have
cruised. Norwich were in freefall, destined to lose their
Premiership status. We were supposedly on the up, yet
Norwich were 2-0 up, with 10 men, after the substitute

referee had send the wrong player from the field. Instead of dismissing defender Spencer Prior, he mistakenly sent off Andy Johnson. It seemed fate was not on our side and defeat against fellow relegation battlers could have sealed out fate.

But something happened. Eight minutes from time, Cottee pulled a goal back and you could visibly see the team fill with confidence. Six minutes later, he grabbed the equaliser and Upton Park went wild. Had there been a few more minutes to play, we may well have grabbed a winner. Norwich were in tatters by the end of the game but West Ham were on a high and, suddenly, you got the impression they could do it.

In the rearranged match at Southampton, Hutchison headed West Ham ahead, only for Neil Shipperley to grab an equaliser. Although we should have won, we gratefully accepted a point away from home, in the knowledge that our next away day was at Aston Villa, a team who were also struggling.

I had volunteered to drive to Villa, as I had my new Orion and felt I owed the gang one. It was just me, Jim Drury and Gary making the trip. What could be simpler? I picked Jim up on the North Circular and we headed off to Redbridge to find Gary. Unfortunately, me and Jim, well, we like a bit of a chinwag, and before I knew where I was, I found myself half-way up the M11.

By the time we got back to Redbridge, Gary was loading his gear back into his brother-in-law's car and was going to make the trip by himself. He was the colour of a large beetroot, not a happy chap. The thought of missing out on sales by being late had done him some serious damage. Things didn't improve as we turned up at The Hawthorns by mistake, adding another 30 minutes to the journey. Still, I think Gary saw the funny side in the end. At least I think he did.

I had a press pass, which confused me as I sat next

to Jim watching West Ham kick from left to right. I then looked up at the monitor to see West Ham kicking from right to left. The cameras are on the other side of the ground, which takes a little bit of getting used to. Moncur scored a brilliant goal in the first half and when Hutch added a second, Jim and I leapt from our seats, much to the chagrin of the watching stewards. Unlike neighbours Coventry, Villa had nothing more exciting in the press box fridge than Müller yoghurt. But then they were much more generous with the points, so I will excuse them on this occasion.

It was a shame that after being on such a high, we had to wait three weeks to get into action again. The win at Villa came on March 18 but our next match, against Nottingham Forest, came on April 8. I went to pick Kev up from his flat in Turnpike Lane before trundling around to Redbridge to meet Gary and young Mark. While waiting for Gary, Kev amused us with stories of a family of vampires he knows in Enfield. This had nothing to do with the fact he'd consumed his first can of wicked strength lager.

Gary turned up 45 minutes late. The Jughunter had been due to drive but hadn't showed. We never saw him again and to this day don't know what happened to him. Gary took over the driving duties and by midday we were having the customary kick-about in the car park. However, when Gary got done for agility and pace by a 10-ton truck, we decided to start selling.

We'd nabbed front row seats, so selling at half time was easy, and in the warm April sunshine we sat down to enjoy the second half. West Ham won a freekick on the edge of the area, which Dicksy curled beautifully into the top corner. I leapt up and started celebrating, turned around and saw thousands of West Ham fans hurtling towards me. I crapped myself, realising how Stanley Baker and Michael Caine must have felt in *Zulu* but at least this lot were friendly. By the time I got back to my seat it was 1-1, Collymore scoring a dubious and undeserved equaliser. Fun point of the day was watching Boere and Stuart Pearce have a pop at each other, real handbags stuff, tripping each other up. Boere may not have been the best striker we ever had, but he was one of the most entertaining to watch off the ball.

The BBC vultures were circling again, tempted by the knowledge that Forest had scored seven the previous week, and it was the same referee who took charge of Manchester United's 9-0 slaughter of Ipswich Town. Sad people. It doesn't work like that.

We drove home happy and I stayed on for a few beers in Kev's local. One of his Arsenal-supporting mates came in. They had a brief chat and Kev promised faithfully not to mention the result of the Arsenal v West Ham match. He turned to me and in a very loud voice said: "So Moncur took this free-kick and Hutch scored a blinder...!"

A curry and a few more beers meant the only place I was sleeping that night was at Kev's flat. He had to be out early because he had tickets for the FA Cup semi-final between Spurs and Everton at Elland Road the next day. The boy is dedicated to his football, I'll give him that.

It was still touch and go but the momentum was with us. We played Wimbledon at Upton Park on the Thursday evening before Good Friday because the District Line was going to be closed over the weekend. Stuart, the QPR fan, joined me for the game, in which we scored a rare home win over the Dons, 3-0, with goals from Dicks, Cottee and Boere.

Ipswich Town were already down when we played them at Portman Road. It was Boere who again saved our blushes with an injury-time strike to grab a point. The stadium was heaving with West Ham fans and while the team may not have deserved a point, the fans certainly did. One defeat in eight matches was the only kind of form that was going to save our necks. The game that made it one defeat in nine was pretty special.

10. Back For Good

West Ham United 2 Blackburn Rovers 0 30.4.95

Champions-elect Blackburn Rovers arrived at Upton Park on a Sunday, another disrupted weekend courtesy of Uncle Rupert. We didn't mind too much at the end of this game, though. Rovers fans filled the lower tier of the Centenary Stand and endured more cries of *Where Were You When You Were Shit?*

Blackburn were odds-on favourites to beat us but Shearer and Co. could not break us down. In the second half Marc Rieper opened his West Ham account with a far post header. The atmosphere inside Upton Park was electric, as Rush broke free and squared the ball for Hutch to score the decisive second goal. West Ham had proved they could live with the best. Survival seemed a formality.

That evening I went to visit an old friend of mine, Emma Jane. We had known each other for many years and I had always fancied her. She was stunningly attractive with a very good figure, and was a lovely girl too. But she'd always had a boyfriend, so I'd never had the chance to ask her out. We sat in her garden drinking coffee and I asked her if there was anyone on the scene.

"As a matter of fact, there is someone I like but he doesn't know yet," she mused. I asked who he was. "I can't tell you," she said, "But you know him." With this, I was really confused, and I hate it when people play guessing games. As I was leaving, I said: "Come on, EJ, who's the lucky fella?" She put her arms around me and smiled as she said: "It's you, you daft bugger!"

She kissed me. I was too stunned to kiss her back. In a way I was pleased. But she just assumed I would be interested. Well, she assumed right, and after I had picked my tongue up from the floor, I kissed her back. Lucky, lucky boy. A model for a girlfriend and West Ham staying up.

After the Blackburn game and a snog with EJ, watching the re-arranged Queens Park Rangers game with Stuart, the QPR fan, was something of an anti-climax. Sorry Stu, but that's just the way it is. A dull 0-0 draw resolved nothing, the only excitement coming when Martin Allen got sent off for a challenge on Rufus Brevett.

The match at Crystal Palace was to be much more eventful. At the time I lived a 10-minute drive from Selhurst Park, so Kev came over to my place and we got seriously hammered before ordering a taxi to take us to the game. It was our worst performance for some time, going down 1-0 to a Chris Armstrong strike. Now things were in the balance again. Kev and I sloped back to the Elmer Lodge and had a few more to drown our sorrows. Now we needed something from games against either Liverpool or Manchester United.

Liverpool came to Upton Park a shadow of the team that had humiliated us so many times in previous years. This time it was our turn. It was hard to take them too seriously when David James stood between the sticks with his bleached blond hair, prompting strains of *He's Got Bird Shit On His Head* to the tune of *Pineapple Head*. We beat them so easily, it was almost embarrassing. Matty Holmes hit the first from a narrow angle, while Hutch scored two more against his old club to secure not only three points, but Premiership status for 1995-96. The relief was visible all around the ground – on the face of Harry Redknapp, the staff, the players and the fans. This had been a real team effort and one that gave everyone an enormous amount of pleasure. More pleasure, dare I say it, than if we had won a cup. We had looked doomed by the end of February, no one gave us a prayer. But we did it.

Now for the players to give the fans some icing on the cake.

11. Some Might Say

West Ham United 1 Manchester United 1 14.5.95

It was EJ's birthday. Fortunately, she was sympathetic to the cause and I was allowed to go and watch the game, despite the fact she was having a barbecue at her place that afternoon. It would still be going by the time I got there.

This match is now enshrined in Upton Park folklore. Quite bizarre really, as we didn't win the game, but the fact it prevented Manchester United winning the title was more precious in the twisted minds of the average West Ham supporter. I can't explain it, no one can, but there is sometimes more pleasure to be had from seeing your most hated rivals lose than there is from seeing your heroes win.

United needed a win from the game and needed Blackburn Rovers to lose or draw at Anfield in their final match. West Ham threw everything at them and it was so sweet when former Man. City player Michael Hughes put West Ham in front in the first half. Up on Merseyside, Shearer scored for Blackburn and it appeared to be all over.

In the second half, though, McClair equalised for Manchester United and Liverpool equalised against Blackburn. United now needed only one more goal for the title. They threw everything at West Ham, including the kitchen sink. Steve Potts and Ludo were both outstanding in keeping United at bay. On the final whistle, a late Jamie Redknapp free-kick had seen

Blackburn lose at Anfield, but United's failure to beat West Ham at Upton Park meant the title went to Ewood Park.

We celebrated like we had won the Cup. It's a bit mean really, I suppose. Rovers winning the title was merely the lesser of two evils. They had bought their way to the championship with owner Jack Walker's millions. At least United, rich as they were, had a lot of home grown talent in their side. But they also had some of our home grown talent, in the shape of Paul Ince, possibly the most obnoxious man in the world.

Not only that, the fact that West Ham had shown such courage was a positive note on which to end the season. We could look forward to 1995-96 in the confident knowledge that what we might lack in ability, we would more than make up for in defiance.

The team paraded around the pitch to rapturous applause, while I ran like the clappers to get back to EJ's house, where the party was almost over. When everyone had gone, she sat astride me on the sofa and made me feel like it was *my* birthday, not hers.

It didn't last of course, these things never do. I had always thought it too good to be true. I'm not sure if it was because I loved football more than her. I don't think so, because she went on to marry her next-door neighbour – a season ticket holder in the Bobby Moore Lower.

After a brief rest, the squad jetted off to Australia for an end-of-season tour, a well-deserved break.

The summer seemed interminable. I took the plunge and bought a season ticket, something I hadn't done since 1990-91, and looked forward to another season of entertaining football. I kept in touch with Kev and Gary, meeting Kev in town for a beer on a couple of occasions, and we discovered we have some overlapping tastes in music. Actually, let me develop that. If our musical tastes were a Venn diagram, there would a tiny intersection where our tastes concur. There is a big enough intersection, though, for us to talk about music and listen into the wee small hours, which probably demonstrates exactly how wide both our musical tastes are in the first place.

Harry's search for a cheap foreign striker appeared to have ended. After taking German Dieter Ekstein on loan the previous April, and finding he couldn't play due to blisters of all things, Harry should have known better. But he didn't. Instead he splashed out £1m on an unknown Dutch striker by the name of Marco Boogers. After laughing myself silly at hearing the name, I did a bit of research and found that the guy actually had a bit of potential. Signed from Sparta Rotterdam, he came with excellent credentials and was reportedly knocking on the door of the Dutch national squad.

My sales manager, Henry, broke the news to me on my mobile while I was out working. I'm always disappointed when friends or colleagues break important news to me about my club, particularly when they support another team, but there you are. Can't be checking Ceefax every five minutes.

The pre-season friendly schedule was hectic and included a game in Germany against TSV Munich 1860, a repeat of the 1965 Cup Winners' Cup final, marking the 30th anniversary of that great match at Wembley. This time, though, the Germans won 4-3. The other pre-season results weren't too bright either. We drew at Bournemouth and won at Exeter, before playing at Oxford on the first weekend in August.

Kev and I decided to go and make a weekend of it. I turned up early on Saturday morning with my tape deck in hand, to copy some of his rare Beatles bootlegs. Within an hour or so, Kev started complaining of stomach cramps but insisted he was well enough to travel.

It was a glorious day, brilliant bright sunshine beating down onto the M40, but by the time we hit Oxford Kev was in a pretty bad way. We thought a pie and a pint – well, a pint anyway – might help to settle Kev's stomach, so we found the nearest pub and ordered some food. Well, the sight of the food made Kev retch and he bolted out the door faster than a rat up a drainpipe. He screamed something about meeting him in Boots, so I stayed put, finished my lunch, my pint, and his pint. I offered his untouched food to a guy standing at the bar and he looked at me like I'd asked him for a blowjob. Some people are just so ungrateful. So I ate Kev's dinner as well.

I found Kev in the local branch of Boots, graphically describing his symptoms to the pharmacist, while waving his arms about like Magnus Pyke on speed. All I could hear was her saying she wasn't a doctor and couldn't diagnose. Kev was looking a bit rough, wearing his oldest denim jacket and I'm sure she thought he was a junkie looking for some kaolin and morphine. Had he told her about the 43 pints of cider he'd consumed in the previous 48 hours, she might have been able to help him. Instead she fobbed him off with a bottle of pink stuff and sent him packing.

I was dubious about the pink medicine but Kev drank it – all of it. It looked like a McDonald's milkshake but Kev said it tasted more like Germoline. He said it was like swallowing a wet tea towel. With Kev being a little delicate, we decided to take seats for the eagerly awaited Oxford Benevolent Cup final.

We got our first glimpse of Mr Boogers and a quite useful looking young Australian by the name of Stan Lazaridis, who wore the number three shirt. Certainly, he got plenty of the ball and every attack seemed to start with him. 2-1 up at half time, I created mental images of an open-top bus ride through the streets of East Ham, proudly parading our new silverware, but of course it was not to be. Paul Moody completed his hat-trick with a real stunner of a volley, which made Kev feel even worse.

I rushed him home – well, maybe rushed is a bit of an exaggeration – but I went as fast as the Orion would go. He went straight to bed, while I raided his video collection and consoled myself with a rerun of Tottenham 1, West Ham 4. Halfway through, Kev reappeared, claiming to feel much better, and started reciting the commentary from the video. I realised that despite being a very sick man, he would live.

I went to Charlton the following Monday to see a Cottee strike edge us a 1-0 win, accidentally taking a wrong turning from the press box and sitting next to the Mayor of Greenwich. He was very polite, though, and Gary's words about looking confident and pretending you should be there were never more prophetic.

The following Saturday I had arranged to cook a meal for The Wonderful Helen at my poky abode (maybe poky isn't the best description, as there had been no 'poky' going on for ages). I hoped that things might change as I trolled around Tesco's for some finest fillet steak and a nice bottle of red.

Kev phoned, bored. The stiffs were playing at Purfleet but I didn't want to go too far, as I had to be back in time for The Wonderful Helen. We looked through the paper. The first division programme was starting a week before the Premiership and my local side, Crystal Palace, were at home to Barnsley. I told Kev if he was prepared to make the trip over to me, we could go. Next thing I knew he was knocking on my door and dragging me down the fire escape to the pub.

The prospect of Palace v Barnsley wasn't that exciting, so we decided to spice the day up by getting pissed and watching the match from the Barnsley end. This proved to be a top decision, as the Barnsley fans overcame their initial hostility to our drunken London accents after assuring them we were West Ham fans who couldn't think of anything else to do on a Saturday afternoon. Palace raced into a 4-1 lead with ace striker Iain Dowie scoring an outrageously offside goal. Barnsley, managed by Danny Wilson, made a brave fightback and got the score to 4-3 but failed to get any more from the game except our sympathy.

Time for a couple more before grooming myself for the impending arrival of The Wonderful Helen. Lovely meal, good company, good wine, and stimulating conversation, but still nothing more. Kev's tip about the ice cubes would have to wait for another day.

With only a few days to go before the start of the 1995-96 campaign, Harry dipped into the transfer market again. Matty Holmes signed for Blackburn in a dramatic deal that saw Robbie Slater and £600,000 come back the other way. I was dubious about the deal. I really liked Matty and wasn't sure about Slater. Lazaridis was also signed in a £300,000 deal and the squad was in place to do battle with Leeds United at Upton Park on the opening day.

Work on *Irrational* was almost complete. All that remained was for a front cover shot to be taken. *Hammers News Magazine* photographer Richard Austin did the business, snapping me and my nephew in the Bobby Moore Lower, along with about 1,000 fellow Hammers fans, as the teams took to the field.

Despite being our most prominent signing for a while, Boogers did not make the starting line-up. Danny Williamson opened our account for the season, only for Tony Yeboah to cancel it out and score a spectacular winner. 2-1 down, Harry turned to our Dutch 'superstar'. He showed some nice touches and good pace but we ended up empty handed again. With away games at Manchester United and Nottingham Forest to come, prospects did not look too good.

There were no tickets for Hammers fans at Old Trafford, due to re-building work, so the match was shown live on big screens at Upton Park. The game will be remembered not for United winning 2-1, or for Steve Bruce becoming our joint top scorer with an hilarious own goal, but for a tackle by Boogers on Gary Neville. Marco had only been on the pitch a few minutes when he went sliding in full pelt on Neville, missing the ball completely and taking away both of the United defender's legs, sending him flying.

Now I never condone bad tackles but this was really funny. Immediately christened "Mad Marco" by the West Ham fans, I felt genuinely sorry for the guy. Here was a man who had signed for a large fee, who had shown a fair degree of skill and commitment in the friendlies he had played in (although I gather he had refused to play in some, hence Redknapp's reluctance to play him from the start.), yet the guy was being asked to turn matches around from losing positions. In my view, he was only trying to show aggression and commitment. It was the last thing Marco Boogers ever did in a West Ham shirt that was noteworthy.

Unfortunately, Gary Neville went on to play for England.

12. Kiss From A Rose

Nottingham Forest 1 West Ham United 1 26.8.95

Two games, no points. Not a disaster – yet. The OLAS
gang for the trip to Forest included a youngster by the
name of Steve, who had taken over from Mark as chief
butt of our twisted humour. It had only been four months
since our last trip to Nottingham, so the scenery all
looked very familiar. Martin Allen put us in front, his last
goal in a Hammers' shirt, but Stuart Pearce equalised for
Forest from the spot soon afterwards. A well earned first
point of the season but the fun was only just about to
start. I had lent Kev my press pass so he could go to the
bar and get a beer. Walking back through the press area,
Frank Clark, the Forest manager, was taking his seat
when he clapped eyes on Kev.

Shaven-headed Kev was resplendent in his scruffy
denim jacket, with Walkman headphones around his
neck, pint of beer in one hand a carrier bag in the other.
Clark took one look at him and said: "You don't look
much like a journalist." Without flinching, and
completely deadpan, Kev replied: "You don't look much
like a football manager." Clark was not impressed and
Kev wisely beat a hasty exit.

Outside I again bumped into Tony 'Mac' who
introduced me to Tony Cottee. TC had agreed to write
the foreword for my book. I don't know if you have ever
met your hero, but I'm afraid I was like a silly giggly
schoolgirl meeting a member of Take That. I can't
remember what I said but it was probably something

pretty dumb, like: "I'm a big fan of yours..." or something equally inane.

We doubled our points tally for the season at home to Tottenham Hotspur. Boss Chris joined me and after detailing him with copious instructions on how not to be recognised as a Totts fan. I slipped off for a half-time piss and left my nephew with him. At the quietest point of the half time break, Mark said to Chris: "You're a Tottenham fan, aren't you?" Nice one, Mark.

Rumours abounded in the press about the situation at West Ham. Harry vehemently denied that Mad Marco was leaving. The names Marcus Stewart and Gareth Taylor had been thrown into the hat, probably by the press, but the one we really hoped wasn't true, the one we hoped was just a bad joke, turned out to be spot on. Iain Dowie re-signed for West Ham just in time to make his second debut in the home match against Chelsea.

Let's put this signing into context. The Premiership was fast heading towards an era where clubs were signing some of the most exciting international talent in the world. We had already splashed out £1m on Boogers but Harry refused to play him. It was obvious we needed some creativity and style, so what did he do? Sign Iain Dowie. This was typical percentage management. Dowie might not have been the most gifted player but adjectives like 'awkward' always sprang to mind. He would give opposition defences 'problems' but not actually score any goals.

Kev and I took his son, Loophead, to see Clive Allen score for the stiffs in a guest appearance at Upton Park on the spare Saturday. The Chelsea game took place on the Monday night and within minutes of kick-off it was clear we were out of our depth. Chelsea raced into a two-goal lead, with our only efforts coming from long range by Dowie. In the second half, Hutch pulled one back with a scrappy header on the goal-line, but the headlines were made by an incident involving Julian Dicks and John Spencer, in which Julian appeared to stamp on Spencer's head. Whether it happened or not was not in question. The blood pouring from the open wound on Spencer's head was proof enough, but the question remained over the intent. It was a cloud that would hang over Dicksy's head for months to come.

It clearly didn't affect Spencer too much. Heavily bandaged, he scored the third and wrapped up a 3-1 Blues victory.

Matt Molloy was a new OLAS writer, who lived quite near Kev, and had started coming along to matches with us. Matt's articles were always seriously funny. He has a wicked sense of humour, so when he told us he'd obtained "top seats" for the Arsenal game, we took it all with a large shovel full of salt.

True to his word, Matt had indeed got us top seats in the second row of the old Clock End at Highbury. Trouble was, it was pissing down and we got soaked. The match was humiliating. By half-time Arsenal had 17 goal attempts to our none, missing a penalty along the way. How the game was still goalless was difficult to see. In the second half, no sooner had Harry seemingly settled for a draw by taking off strikers and packing the defence and midfield, than Dicks was sent off for a reckless foul on Ian Wright. Wright scored with his second penalty attempt.

Worse was to follow. With Moncur leaving the field through injury, and both outfield substitutes used, Harry was forced to throw on goalkeeper Les Sealey as an outfield player. Drenched through to the skin, losing a London derby and seeing your reserve goalkeeper playing up front, has to be one of the worst things that can happen to any football fan. But we made the most of if, singing *We All Agree, Sealey Is Better than Bergkamp*. Defeat left us with six league matches played, no wins and only two points. Panic mode was about to set in.

Kev and I went out to drown our sorrows that night but I think I over-did it a bit. As my head hit the pillow the room started spinning and I knew instantly what was going to happen. I ran to the bathroom and deposited my curry in the sink, only it refused to disappear. Despite much poking around, it still refused to shift. Still very drunk, I pulled the pedestal from under the basin, fetched a bowl from the kitchen and undid the U-bend to clear the blockage, then replaced the pedestal. In my drunken state, though, I had replaced the pedestal upside down. It was something Kev only spotted when he came to sell the flat! Even so, I was proud of my DIY capabilities.

The Coca-Cola Cup offered some light relief. We had drawn Bristol Rovers away in the first leg, which meant a trip not to Bristol, but to Bath. In a logistics exercise the scale of D-Day, two cars formed the official OLAS posse, the first leaving from OLAS Towers containing Gary, John, the Seller, young Steve, and new OLAS writer Darren Jones. The second car, departing from North London, contained Kev, Matt and Buzz, another friend of the fanzine, famous throughout the Bobby Moore Stand for his big hair. After searching for hours for a pub, it was almost kick-off time. Moncur scored the only goal of the game with a swirling 25-yarder, apparently. Buzz had just bought some chips and we were all tucking in when the goal went in, so we missed it. Still, it gave us our first victory of the season and must have lifted spirits slightly.

After the game Gary and I interviewed Rovers' striker Marcus Stewart, who poured cold water on the idea that he might be coming to West Ham. Just as well, we thought, after seeing his performance.

13. You Are Not Alone

West Ham United 2 Everton 1 23.9.95

The first league win of the season came at the
seventh attempt. Succeeding where we had failed the
season before, we managed to hold on to a lead against
Everton, provided courtesy of two Dicksy penalties.
Jules had been charged with bringing the game into
disrepute after the Spencer incident and showed good
character to come back and score twice from the spot.
Being a Bristolian, he'd also had to endure a lot of stick
from the Rovers fans the previous Wednesday. For once,
his temperament seemed to hold.

Another point was gathered at The Dell, in a battling
0-0 draw shown live by that nice man, Uncle Rupert.
This was the second game of the season I missed but it
turned out to be the last. Two days later, a seemingly
more confident West Ham saw off Bristol Rovers 3-0,
Cottee scoring his long overdue first goal of the season
after Dicks and Bishop had put West Ham 2-0 up in the
second half. The performance was helped by the return
of Hughes, who had returned to Strasbourg but was
now back for a second loan spell.

Another live game from Uncle Rupert followed. West
Ham's good form continued with a 1-0 victory at
Wimbledon, Cottee doubling his total for the season and
shooting us up the table to the lofty heights of 13th
place.

On the 19th, *An Irrational Hatred of Luton* was
published, and the first supplies were available at

Independent UK Sports' offices, just off Tottenham Court Road. I was supposed to be out working with my sales manager, Henry, but if the truth were told, he was as excited about it as I was, and he drove up to London with me so I could collect my first batch of copies hot off the press. I got my first taste of stardom, being cornered by virtually every member of staff for a signed copy. I thoroughly enjoyed it and found it difficult to get through the door, my head was so big. After the initial excitement had passed the important job of actually shifting copies got under way. I put up posters all down Green Street before the Blackburn Rovers game to inform the public the book was available, and stood sheepishly next to Gary with about 50 copies. To my amazement, we sold them all within an hour.

Was I pleased? Almost as pleased as I was to see Dowie score his first goal for West Ham in his second spell, with a looping header from a perfect 'Bish' cross. The lead should have doubled but for a misunderstanding between Cottee and Dowie, and it proved costly as Shearer nicked a last minute equaliser. Disappointed as I was to see the lead go, and so late on too, I could not be deflated after the apparent success of *Irrational*. Now I could see it was selling, the question was, would people like it?

I would have to wait for a definitive answer to that question. In the meantime I drove Gary and Marc Williams, editor of *On the Terraces* fanzine, down to The Dell for our third round Coca-Cola Cup clash with Southampton. It was a poor game, Southampton taking the lead after a shot from Barry Venison was cruelly deflected. We should have earned at least a replay when Cottee scrambled an equaliser but Shipperley scored the winner for Saints with a spectacular diving header and, for once, we went out of the Cup to a team from the same league. Harry was philosophical in the press conference, just as we were on the trip home. After all, it was the league that really mattered in these high-pressure days. While in the past we might have looked for mere survival in the league and concentrated on trying to win a Cup, with the money involved, Premiership survival had become the be-all and end-all. Both cup competitions were beginning to pale into insignificance.

I had dropped a few copies of the book around at various radio stations and was genuinely surprised to receive a phone call from the producer of *Drive,* the early evening show on *Radio Five*, then presented by John Inverdale. They invited me in to talk about the book and what it means to be a West Ham fan. John was very kind and put my nerves at ease. But, inevitably, and rather disappointingly, he highlighted a paragraph in the book describing crowd trouble.

Don't get me wrong, I was very glad of the publicity, but it seems a shame that the only reason some books seem to sell is if they sensationalise the seedier side of football supporting. Events at Euro 2000 reinforce my point. Where were the camera crews before the Portugal game, when English and Portuguese fans drank happily together without a hint of trouble? Those people who get hard-ons reading the books of Doug and Eddie Brimson will no doubt hate this book But then its not aimed at them. I did receive a few comments like: "Not much about the crowd violence in it, was there?"

I could not then, and do not understand now, where these people are coming from.

Inverdale was a charming host. Gary had challenged me beforehand to work the current OLAS buzz-word, "Chipper", into the interview. When Inverdale asked me why I hated Luton, I told him five or six reasons and added: "Altogether, not very chipper people really."

The following Saturday came a chance to improve on

our appalling record at Hillsborough. I went up on the Friday night and stayed with Lucy, sampling the delights of the Sheffield nightlife. I'd got three tickets, Lucy joining me at the game, together with her boyfriend Martin. Wednesday hit all parts of the goal except the back of the net, allowing West Ham to scrape a win with a scuffed Dowie shot that trickled painfully under the body of 'keeper Pressman. Had Dowie made proper contact, no doubt it would have gone for a throw-in. As Kev said later in an OLAS article: "Pressman was beaten, not by the pace of the shot, but by the lack of it!" The wooden seats in the upper tier of the Leppings Lane end clattered with delight throughout the second half as we hung on for the kind of dodgy victory synonymous with visiting teams at Upton Park.

We weren't complaining, though, a fifth league match unbeaten saw us in 12th place, our highest league position for eight years, and talk of relegation was replaced, for the time being, with talk of a push for Europe.

14. Wonderwall

West Ham United 1 Aston Villa 4 4.11.95

Ever heard the expression, crashing back down to earth with a bump? This was just one of those games when nothing went right. Villa scored some spectacular goals and by the time West Ham started playing it was far too late. A Dicks penalty was scant reward for the effort shown by the majority of the players. Even Boogers got a run out, so Harry must have been desperate.

The following Monday I attended the launch of Tony Cottee's book, *Claret & Blues*, which Independent UK Sports also used as an opportunity to officially release my book. This was a chance to meet Tony properly and have a good chat, not giggle like a pre-pubescent schoolgirl, as I had done before. The afternoon went really well. Gary and the other fanzine editors had also been invited and we virtually monopolised Tony's attention for the entire afternoon. We couldn't get him to spill any juicy beans, though.

With England playing a friendly against Switzerland the following Wednesday, the blank Saturday was taken up by Alvin Martin's second testimonial. Not many players are granted testimonials these days and it's even rarer in the atmosphere of the modern game for a player to receive two. Some say that for a player of the stature of Martin it is almost an insult to the fans to have to fork out for a guy who already earns considerably more than they do. I tend to sympathise with this view. Benefit matches, such as those held for Gerhardt Ampofo in 1986, a young player whose promising career had been cut short through injury, are possibly more deserving cases. Or indeed for a player like George Parris, a loyal servant to West Ham who I would bet never earned much more than £600 a week at the very peak of his career. But then Georgie had a testimonial in April 1995 – and only 1,379 turned up. So what does that tell you?

Whatever your view on testimonials, 8,710 turned up to witness Alvin's, myself and Stuart, the QPR fan, included. We saw a good game, which ended 3-3 with Danny Williamson, Boogers and Hutchison scoring. Guesting for West Ham that afternoon were Jamie Redknapp, Steve McManaman and Chris Waddle. It should have been a combination to die for but, to be honest, they looked cack.

In OLAS we had been calling for Williamson to be recalled to the side for some time. We felt Danny had been overlooked and had never let the side down when he had played. He got his opportunity at Bolton, where West Ham fans also got the rare chance to watch a Premiership game from some ropey terracing, just like the old days.

It was freezing cold and my bedclothes were like cardboard (but that had nothing to do with the weather) as I left the flat at 7.30am and coaxed the Orion into life. I picked up Darren in East Ham, now an OLAS regular and christened "The Tortoise." Darren has a wicked sense of humour and superb comic timing when it comes to telling jokes. He had us all in stitches as Kev drove us up to Burnden Park, the time just flashing by. Matt was following us up with fiancée, Helen (not The Wonderful Helen, but lovely just the same). We took up a parking space in the mud patch outside the away entrance. Matt came hurtling towards us at great speed, applied the handbrake at the last minute and spun his car around into a perfectly parallel parking position. He left some huge skid marks – and not just on the ground, I can tell you. "Cor, that was f*@@!!!g lucky!" he said, emerging rather sheepishly from his Mondeo, while we looked on ashen-faced. We used Helen and her regional accent to get us into a pub which seemed to be caught in a time warp, with beer about 15p a pint and decent grub. I bought a round and got the barmaid to check she'd got it right.

The first half of the game was notable for nothing except the unprecedented amount of tutting and swearing coming from the West Ham fans. In the second half, Ian Bishop marked his 200th appearance for the Hammers with a sweetly-struck shot to make it 1-0. Cottee added a second soon afterwards with a close-range effort that appeared to take a deflection. Then, near the end, Williamson picked up the ball on the edge of our area, ran the entire length of the pitch and scored with a crisp, accurate shot that sent the standing fans behind the goal into raptures.

It also put a smile on the faces of those at OLAS Towers who had been calling for his inclusion.

Something else put a smile on my face too. Whilst milling about outside the press room waiting for Harry to turn up, I felt a tap on my shoulder. It was Cottee. "Hello Rob," he beamed. I nearly fell over. He remembered my name! I couldn't think what to say and so, in traditional fashion, when flummoxed, went for the insult. "You're not claiming that goal, are you?" I said. Fortunately he saw the funny side.

In the press conference, Harry launched into a verbal attack on the Bolton fans seated behind him, claiming he had never heard such abuse. One of the hacks asked him if he was in fear of his safety. "Nah," he said, "I had Frank Burrows with me."

Harry claimed not to be surprised by the margin of the

victory. After all, apart from one hiccup against Villa, we were unbeaten since September 16. It was just as well, because a nightmare sequence of fixtures and results was about to unfold through December and January, and we were going to have to live off the fat gathered in the preceding months.

15. Father And Son

Blackburn Rovers 4 West Ham United 2   2.12.95

Two home matches produced four points. Liverpool played out a goalless draw, which was entertaining enough, but only sticks in my memory because Pottsy nearly scored his second goal for West Ham in 10 years. Struggling QPR visited on the Saturday and were unfortunate to lose to a Cottee strike mid-way through the second half. Stuart, the QPR fan, predicted relegation for the Superhoops and he was to be proved correct.

Meanwhile West Ham faced a nightmare spell with five of the next six matches away from home. Not just away from home, but a long way from home. We didn't know it at the time but due to postponements, that was the way it panned out. The sequence began with a trip to Ewood Park. Almost a year on from our heroic 4-2 defeat to the champions-elect, we suffered another defeat by the same score that was anything but heroic. Shearer grabbed another hat-trick and Mike Newell the other as Rovers romped into a 4-0 lead. Robbie Slater, playing against his old club, and Dicks from the penalty spot, added a bit of respectability to the scoreline but only after Mad Marco had taken to the field. I was starting to quite like him. Pity he never played again. He reportedly sloped off back to his caravan in Holland, claiming mental stress, and was never seen again, although he was allegedly still on the pay roll as recently as last Thursday.

Matty Holmes had sorted us out tickets to the game plus players' bar passes. Matty had always been a great supporter of OLAS and we had always championed his cause. A truly nice bloke, Matty's move to Blackburn Rovers was something of a mystery. Ray Harford allegedly bought him thinking he was a winger but one day in training said to Matty: "You're not a winger, are you?" to which Matty replied "No, who told you that?" The relationship slid gradually downhill from that point. Matty recently had to retire from the professional game through injury but is still doing the business at non-league level for Dorchester Town. Good luck, mate.

In the players' bar after the game there were no players worth interviewing. Kev went and stood next to Shearer (as I said, no players worth interviewing), so I decided to interview Kev instead. "Kev, you seem to make a habit of coming to shite away grounds and getting stuffed..." "Yes, well I'm standing next to Alan Shearer, who is an arrogant little..." we stopped the interview there.

I had another quick chat with my new mate Tony Cottee and asked if, at some point, I could do a lengthy interview with him for OLAS. He agreed and gave me his phone number. I'd pulled! I was having more success getting Premiership players to give me their home phone numbers than I was with women, so I thought I might as well go for it. After searching in vain on the way home for a chippy that wasn't run by Chinese people (that's not a racist slur, they just can't cook proper chips, can they?), we steadied ourselves for another long away trip on a Monday night, this time to Everton.

This was possibly the lowest turn out of West Ham fans I have ever seen at an away game but it was understandable. Liverpool on a Monday night, probably with work the next morning and with the game live on telly, what would you rather do? Well, secretly I would rather have stayed at home too but I was on a roll, and wanted to keep it going. Another heavy defeat ensued. Everton were nothing special once again but turned us over 3-0 thanks largely to a Graham Stuart goal that took a huge deflection, Ludo getting sent off and Julian Dicks going in goal. Jules could do nothing about the penalty but for the rest of the game played a blinder, even keeping out the returning hero, Duncan Ferguson. Everton managed only one more goal, so on the face of it, a 3-0 defeat wasn't too bad.

Joe Royle was diplomatic in the press conference but Harry was seething. Poor Ludo had never been sent off in his career before and Harry felt he hadn't deserved it. Still, rules are rules and unless you're a big club, that's the way it goes.

Relief arrived in the shape of the visit of Southampton and a 2-1 victory. Bishop had put the visitors ahead with an own goal, but goals from Cottee and Dowie wrapped it up in the second half and sent us off to our Christmas drinks in fine fettle. One more game to negotiate before Christmas, as the ridiculous fixture computer paired us with Middlesbrough at The Riverside on the day before Christmas Eve. The weather was atrocious and several calls were made on the way up to check the game was still going ahead. Unfortunately it was and we had to keep going. Gary's sound system blasted out *What's The Story, Morning Glory?* by *Oasis* all the way there and all the way back; a mind-numbing mantra that served to dull the pain of yet another away defeat at the hands of a team only marginally better than us. Again we were 4-0 down before we had found our feet, Dicks and Cottee this time adding a couple of meaningless goals.

Rumours were flying at this time about some more signings, in particular, the Croatian defender Slaven Bilic who, allegedly, had single handedly dragged Karlsrühe, of the German Bundesliga, from relegation material to

UEFA Cup contenders. Harry denied it in the press conference, so we all knew it must be true.

The 100th edition of OLAS hit the stands on Boxing Day. Unfortunately the game, a home match against Coventry City, was called off due to a frozen pitch. In true West Ham tradition, I had arrived at the ground, having treated my dad to a ticket, only to find out about the postponement when within 100 yards of the main gate.

A similar fate befell the home match with Newcastle United on December 30, so me and Kev went to watch Wimbledon beat Arsenal at Highbury instead. We didn't take in another game until New Year's Day, the trip to Maine Road.

Somehow I ended up driving again. Gary had tossed a coin at his end of the phone and assured me he'd won fair and square. I held a New Year's Eve party and had to step over several bodies on my way out, leaving them a note to shut the door behind them as they left.

The Orion was starting to protest at the number of long away trips and on leaving the M6, the gearbox started making noises like the mating call of the dromedary camel (so I'm told). The official supporters' car park looked far too far away for our liking, so we drove around for a while, waited 'till no one was looking and sneaked into the Kippax Stand car park. Job done.

The news on the street was that with Ludo suspended, Les Sealey had been due to play in goal but had torn a hamstring in training. Harry had tried to loan a replacement in time but had been unsuccessful, so 17-year-old Neil Finn was to be thrust into his debut. You would have thought with a rookie stuck between the sticks, the defence would have pulled out all the stops to protect him. Think again. Niall Quinn capitalised on Rieper's error and clipped the ball over Finn to open the scoring. The West Ham fans, probably still drunk from

New Year celebrations, sang *Finn Finnery, Finn Finnery, Finn Finn Ferooo, Our 'Keeper's Sixteen And He Should Be At School.*

In the second half, Dowie levelled the scores but once again we snatched defeat from the jaws of victory, Quinn scoring a second towards the end. We waited outside to try and catch the players for some interviews. John Moncur, who hadn't had the best game of his life, came barging through, ignoring all requests for an autograph, saying he was in a hurry. Frank Worthington appeared on the steps and suddenly Moncs had all the time in the world. Funny that. Worthington still cuts a fine figure and has a lot of class, even if he did look a bit of a twat in that fedora.

I got home at midnight to find the place exactly as I had left it. The lazy bastards hadn't even picked up the empty cans on the floor. Tired and depressed, I left that job for tomorrow.

16. Missing

West Ham United 0 Manchester United 1   22.1.96

The FA Cup offered our only real chance of glory and a third round tie at home to Southend United looked a formality on paper. Fortunately it was a formality on grass, too. After stubborn resistance, principally from 'keeper Simon Royce, Southend finally succumbed to goals from Hughes and Moncur. Hutchison, largely out of favour in recent months, completed a £1.2m move to Sheffield United and while he never set the world on fire at West Ham, I was sorry to see him go. Transfer activity came thick and fast. Peter Shilton was signed as goalkeeping cover and Chris Whyte joined on loan. It was hard to keep track of all the comings and goings at Chadwell Heath, where a bewildering number of players were given trials.

With the cup diversion out of the way it was back on the road again, this time to Leeds, who by happy coincidence, had just re-signed Lee Chapman on loan, so this promised to be amusing. Chapman was his usual angular, bumbling self but it was a shock to everyone when he got himself sent off for elbowing Marc Rieper. He'd never shown anything like that sort of aggression when playing for West Ham. It wasn't a surprise, however, when the podgy, little Swede, Tomas Brolin, scored twice to condemn West Ham to yet another defeat.

I smuggled The Tortoise into the press conference and briefed him on procedure. "Whatever you do, don't make eye contact with Howard Wilkinson," I warned him. "And for God's sake, don't ask Harry anything about Boogers – It makes him twitch." Darren nodded and zipped up his jacket to hide his West Ham shirt from view. No sooner had the first pregnant pause arrived in Harry's press conference, than Darren piped up: "Has Boogers still got a chance, Harry?" Redknapp visibly went a deep shade of purple. "He's Injured." he retorted. "But yeah, he's still in with a chance, for sure, for sure..."

The arrival of Slaven Bilic had been confirmed a couple of weeks earlier but he couldn't play until a work permit had come through. Rumours also abounded that West Ham were trying to sign Romanian World Cup '94 star Ilie Dumitrescu from Tottenham. This concerned me. Sure, Dumitrescu was a big name with a big reputation, but he couldn't get a game at Spurs, and they were shit. So what did that say about him? Dumitrescu did sign, of course, a few days before we were due to face Manchester United at Upton Park. But guess what? He needed a new work permit and it looked unlikely he was going to get one.

Uncle Rupert intervened once more and moved our game with United to the Monday. A terrific match was settled by a strike from Eric Cantona but West Ham deserved so much more from the game. Bishop had a goal-bound shot cleared off the line by Dennis Irwin, who appeared from nowhere, and Dowie hit the bar in a game that saw Nicky Butt sent off for a scandalous challenge on Dicks. Exciting it may have been, but the fact remained we had gathered only three points from a possible 21.

It didn't matter too much, though. We were about to collect 15 from a possible 15.

17. Spaceman

Tottenham Hotspur 0 West Ham United 1 12.2.96

Remember what I said about turning points in a
season? Just when things were starting to look a little
grim, Harry pulled out the signing of the decade with the
purchase of Bilic. Although he signed on January 5 and
could not play until February 12, it is possible that his
positive, never-say-die attitude had started to rub off on
the players before he had even set foot on the pitch. If
ever there was a turning point in season 1995-96, this
was it.

We beat Coventry City 3-2 at Upton Park to end an
awful sequence of results. Dowie scored the winner after
the Sky Blues had come back from 2-0 down to
equalise, and all seemed lost. Frank Lampard Junior,
performing miracles as captain of the youth team,
stepped onto the Upton Park turf as a first team player
for the first time. The youth team were to go on and win
the South-East Counties title that year and lose in the
final of the FA Youth Cup to a Liverpool team containing
a certain Michael Owen.

Meanwhile, things were happening away from football
too. I had been so wrapped up in my football, I had
almost forgotten about life outside. Work was
depressing me, as I found it hard to meet the standards
expected. Not just because of the area I was covering,
but due to my own timid approach to the job. I had been
finding it very hard to put programmes of calls together
for my sales manager. I was living in a cold, poky little

flat and, apart from my cat, Ludo, had very little company. It was probably for that reason that I immersed myself so fully in my football, but it was clear that I wasn't happy.

After returning from work one night, trying to make appointments for my sales manager and myself, I had experienced a whole evening of rejections. My sister was moving house and needed a new endowment policy and I had provisionally arranged to go and see her the next day. I called her to check it was still okay, only to be informed she had already signed up elsewhere. That was the final straw. In my cold, desolate flat I broke down. My sister, detecting that I had been upset earlier, called me back and caught me blubbing. She came over immediately and we chatted about how I could improve things.

Fate dealt a hand when my friend, Mark, inherited a house from his mother and found himself rattling around in a four-bedroom semi in Bexley. Being unemployed, he could use some extra income and suggested I take one of the bedrooms. I ripped his arm off. At least I had somewhere warm and comfortable to stay now, as well as some human contact outside of work. I'd almost given up with women – all those I wanted were either unavailable or just playing plain hard to get, so I immersed myself even deeper into my football.

The weekend before I moved, Christina, my pen pal from Nottingham, came down to stay for the weekend. West Ham were playing at home to Nottingham Forest, so I bought a couple of tickets, let Matt use my season ticket and phoned Tony Cottee to ask him if I could wangle a couple of players' bar passes. Not a problem. Chris came down on the Friday night and we sat and talked over old times, looking through photo albums. On the Saturday we made it early to the Boleyn Ground, popped in at our new regular watering hole, The Millers

Well, then watched West Ham beat Forest 1-0 with a goal from Robbie Slater.

Chris had grown out of her football but I was at least able to fulfil an 11-year long promise, to take her to a game at Upton Park. We didn't have long to hang about in the players' bar. Not long enough to wait for TC to come out so we could thank him anyway, as we had tickets for a West End show and had to get weaving. A lovely weekend was rounded off with a trip to the Tower of London on the Sunday and the realisation that Nottingham wasn't exactly the other side of the planet, and more regular visits might be in order.

After two good league wins it was perhaps only natural that we should stumble against first division opponents in the FA Cup. The draw had already been made and we knew a win would give us a fifth round tie at Stamford Bridge. Whether it was that affecting the performance, I'm not sure, but Grimsby Town player-manager Brian Laws scored the opener before Dowie equalised and that was the end of the scoring. It meant a replay at Blundell Park, Cleethorpes, on St. Valentine's Day.

Meanwhile, more transfer dealings had brought the talented young Portuguese star Daniel Da Cruz Carvalho, or Dani to his mates, to Upton Park on loan until the end of the season. Dani made his debut as a substitute against Forest but made his first full start against Tottenham at White Hart Lane on a Monday night for Uncle Rupert. Bilic also made his debut in a game that will live long in the memory of all those who witnessed it. My boss, Chris, had got a ticket with me in the West Ham end, along with John Fuller, manager of the Chichester office and a lifelong Hammers fan. As everyone was standing anyway, we all stood together, ignoring our seat numbers, to see Dani score in the fifth minute to set up a morale-boosting victory. Cottee and

Dowie could have made it four between them by the end of the night, we were that dominant. We bumped into Matt's sister, or "Matista" as we know her, the black sheep of the family being a Tottenham fan, and we gave her a deserved hard time.

Being a West Ham fan though, is not all wine and roses. Oh no. With Bilic, Hughes and Dani all ineligible for the replay at Grimsby, it was a very different squad that made the trip to Cleethorpes.

It was a very familiar OLAS squad that made the trip, however. John, the Seller, was driving Gary, Kev and me. John is a very affable bloke and he seems to be quite friendly with a lot of lorry drivers. At almost every roundabout, one of them would flash their lights at him and give him a cheery wave. What top blokes!

I'd never had the pleasure of visiting Cleethorpes before and we soon got lost trying to find the ground. Our usual trick is to ask the nearest pretty girl and while driving past the sports centre we spotted a tasty looking blonde walking ahead of us, so we pulled up to ask directions. This 'lady' turned round to reveal an Adams apple the size of a golf ball and designer stubble George Michael would have been proud of. "It's back up that way by McDonald's," he, she or it growled and we scarpered pronto. Kev and I decided to sample the local cuisine, ordering some sublime haddock and chips. It was mid-February on the North Sea coast, yet all the locals were wandering around in tee-shirts without so much as a stiff nipple, playing 'spot the soft Southerner.'

Less said about the game, the better. We lost 3-0. End of story. It's the West Ham fan's eternal dilemma – we can beat Tottenham at White Hart Lane one minute, then get turned over by a bunch of enthusiastic amateurs the next.

The next morning I had to do an interview on BBC Three Counties Radio, who had picked up on the fact that I had written a book that was mildly disrespectful to Luton and wanted a chat. What they didn't tell me was they had the chairman of the Luton Town Supporters' Club on the other line. He was quite gentle with me, though, and I came out of it reasonably unscathed.

The yo-yo nature of the West Ham fan's being was graphically illustrated the following Saturday, when we beat Chelsea 2-1 at Stamford Bridge. Gavin Peacock put Chelsea ahead but goals from Dicks and Williamson shut up the Chelsea fans, while we told them exactly what they could do with their blue flag. It was a particularly sweet victory for Dicksy, who had suffered criticism in the press from David Mellor and who, in my view, had been treated very unfairly by Chelsea boss Glenn Hoddle, who had allegedly refused to allow John Spencer to speak in Julian's defence at his hearing.

Mad Marco was finally offloaded, albeit on loan to Dutch side FC Groningen. I was annoyed. I felt he hadn't been given a fair crack of the whip.

A fifth consecutive league victory came courtesy of leaders Newcastle United's visit to Upton Park. Williamson and Cottee scored in a pulsating 2-0 victory that ate into Newcastle's lead at the top and revived Manchester United's hopes of snatching the Premiership title.

It had to be Arsenal who ended the run. Boring bloody, Arsenal, who turned up, hit a goal in the second minute through John Hartson, then shut up shop in that really irritating way that Arsenal do. We did get a penalty but Dicks, suffering concussion, made a rare miss. Boring and Lucky Arsenal. Dinner with The Wonderful Helen was by now the best I could expect and I was happy to accept it on the basis that if I was in her face, she might change her mind.

At Coventry, a pulsating first half finished 2-2 after Cottee had put us ahead. Salako and Whelan put

Coventry 2-1 up and Rieper equalised. The scoring dried up in the second half, but by now we were travelling to matches not expecting to get beaten. It was a very peculiar feeling.

Dumitrescu's work permit finally turned up in the post and he was able to make his debut against Middlesbrough at Upton Park. 'Boro 'keeper Gary Walsh gifted an opener to Dowie, while Dicksy made sure from the spot. Harry was upbeat in the press conference, on top form. Winning clearly agreed with him.

18. Don't Look Back In Anger

Newcastle United 3 West Ham United 0 18.3.96

The next time you hear a West Ham fan complaining about the lack of TV coverage we receive, remind him of this fact: during season 1995-96, we appeared live on Sky TV on no fewer than seven occasions. This was a complete pain in the arse, as the majority of the games were away, on a Monday night. Newcastle away on a Monday night was a challenge that had to be done, just for the heck of it, not for any other reason.

I shared the driving with Matt in his Mondeo and we found a convenient spot to park, just by the Strawberry pub. A local lad leapt out and offered to mind the car. "That's all very well," Matt said in his most reasonable QS manner, "but what if a bunch of big lads came and started messing with my car? What would you do then?"

"Easy," said the urchin "I'd kick their fucking heads in!" We thought he had a good point, so Matt gave him a quid.

More goalkeeping problems meant that Les Sealey finally got to make his Hammers debut – but it was not a happy one. We were trounced – and I mean murdered – 3-0, with a sending off for Pottsy, of all people, for good measure. It's a long way home from Newcastle at the best of times but starting the journey at 10pm on a Monday night would not be my first choice.

The visit of Manchester City the following Saturday provided much more entertainment. Dowie put us 1-0 up before Keith Curle missed a penalty. Dowie added a second, Quinn pulled one back, but Dicksy added a pile-driving third. Dani skipped through the penalty area and slotted home the fourth from a narrow angle. Quinn scored a consolation with the last kick of the game but City were doomed.

Around this time, with work really getting me down, I was looking around for another job. Stuart, the QPR fan, worked for Barclays Bank and pointed out a vacancy within their life section, setting up and editing the in-house magazine. It was a job I would have killed for, combining my new-found knowledge of the financial services industry with magazine editing and production. I had an initial interview, produced a portfolio and waited. Over semi-final weekend I took the opportunity to visit Christina in Nottingham and sample the delights of The Castle – the oldest pub in the world – and Sherwood Forest among others.

Over Easter, a hectic schedule began with a 1-1 draw with Wimbledon, those two, fine cultured players Dicks and Vinny Jones scoring the goals. On Easter Monday we travelled to Anfield more in hope than expectation, seeking our first win there since 1963. Phil drove his new Rover, offering us a choice: fast and expensive, or slow and cheap. The season was pretty meaningless by now. We were not in any danger of being relegated and it showed in our disinterested performance at Anfield, going down 2-0. I waited with The Tortoise by the players' exit for Gary and Phil to emerge, and we watched the players file out one by one onto the coach with VIP painted on its side. I was confused. What could VIP possibly stand for? For these were not important people. Darren suggested it might stand for 'Very Ineffective Players'. It was hard to be too critical, though. For the second season running the players had pulled us out of a hole – admittedly, a hole they had dug for themselves, but nonetheless they had done it, and provided plenty of entertainment along the way.

Bolton Wanderers came and went, a Cottee goal pushing them closer to the division from whence they came, and a trip to Villa Park was memorable only for the debut of the famous 'rhubarb and custard' kit. We wondered who on earth would be seen dead in a magnolia shirt, a colour we were later informed by the powers that be, was called 'ecru.' Fine. The match finished 1-1, Dani sliding a delicious through-ball to Cottee to equalise Paul McGrath's opener. The visit to QPR was notable only for the fact that me, Kev and Matt all sat together in the upper tier of the School End, wearing our Croatia shirts, a tribute to the great Slaven Bilic. Naturally, having forked out £40 each for the shirt, he proceeded to play like an utter tosser and we lost 3-0. Still, the win was not enough to keep Rangers up, but Stuart, the QPR fan, was able to spot us in our shirts from his seat in the Ellerslie Road stand, and gave us a cheery wave. I think it was a wave, anyway.

The season ended with a 1-1 draw against Sheffield Wednesday, Dicks finding the net yet again, and young Rio Ferdinand making his first team debut as a substitute.

Despite the season petering out in a disappointing fashion, the future was still looking bright. We finished 10th, our highest finish for 10 years, the youth team swept all before them, with the exception of Liverpool in the FA Youth Cup final, but their season had produced a run of 18 successive victories and provided the first team with two new debutants. New signings Bilic and Dumitrescu more than made up for the disappointment of the Boogers fiasco. Now we all needed a break. For Kev and me, that took the form of Matt's stag weekend in Dublin. And Euro 96.

19. Oooh Ahhhh, Just a Little Bit

England 4 Holland 1 18.6.96

The job with Barclays didn't come off. I was disappointed. I had felt the time for a move was right. As it happened, a move of sorts did come about. I was offered a change of agency within the CIS. Same job, different area. After mulling it over for a while I decided to go for it. I had a new sales manager, Alan, who drove me very hard, and by the end of the year I was second in the office for sales. It seemed at least the work front was sorting itself out but not before one of the auditors had presented me with a bill for £350 after a miscalculation on my accounts.

Matt had decided to get married and was having a stag weekend in Dublin. Kev and I came along, together with about 20 of his other mates, and put a serious drain on local supplies of Guinness. Neither Kev nor I are the clubbing type, so we left the others to it on the Friday night and just concentrated on taking in the local atmosphere.

The others rolled in at about 4am, very much the worse for wear, Matt having had his jacket stolen, wallet and credit cards included. The next day, a young lady who had found his cards had rung Helen back in London to let her know. Potentially embarrassing. The next day Kev and I found the only protestant pub in Dublin and watched Rangers beat Hearts in the Scottish Cup final. The Irish rugby team were playing the Barbarians at Lansdowne Road and it was Eurovision Song Contest night, which seems to mean a lot more in Ireland than it does here, probably because they stand a chance of winning it. Ireland did win, as I recall. Certainly, the young lady I was snogging on the bridge was very happy about something.

Someone had been spiking Matt's drinks and, by 9pm, he was slaughtered. Five of us dragged him back to the hotel, with him singing at the top of his voice: *Who The Fuck Are Man United?*

We reminded him of it later, and it didn't seem to embarrass him at all. A more leisurely Sunday and, just to prove what a small world it is, who should get on the same plane as us at Dublin but Jim 'Morrissey' Drury. He told us the bad news about the kids losing the second leg of the FA Youth Cup final at Anfield. Frank Lampard had scored in the first minute to make it 2-1 on aggregate but Liverpool ran out 2-1 winners on the night, 4-1 on aggregate.

Euro 96 had been eagerly anticipated since the end of the 1994 World Cup. England, as hosts, had qualified automatically and a string of friendlies had not really provided any true guide to form. The tournament provided more interest for us Hammers fans than just watching England. In fact, with no West Ham players in the Three Lions' squad, it was almost more interesting to watch Marc Rieper playing for Denmark and Slaven Bilic playing for Croatia. An injured Ilie Dumitrescu failed to appear for Romania. I watched England's opening match against Switzerland at my parents' house in Hastings. Disappointed after all the pomp and ceremony and a great goal from Shearer, we could only draw the game 1-1.

Work on the new agency started on June 10, just as I learned I had successfully passed my Financial Planning Certificate at the first attempt – a relief, as I'd had a spot of bother with exams until that point.

England took on Scotland at Wembley in what was billed as an all-important group decider, the Scots having earned a battling 0-0 draw with Holland in their opening game. As ever, it was sweet to beat the Scots. They will never let you forget when they win, but always conveniently ignore the result when they lose, blaming the ref, the pitch, or cloud formations – anything but admit they are actually crap. Holland beat Switzerland, so our match with the Dutch was likely to decide the group winners.

I had arranged to watch the game with Kev at a pub in Potters Bar, along with a dozen or so of his colleagues who had formed a fantasy football league throughout the season. By sticking a fiver each away every month, we had plenty of dosh for a few beers and a slap-up curry. We arrived at the pub just as Spain v Romania was finishing, so by the time the England match started we were already steaming. Possibly the best England performance since the 1990 World Cup semi-final followed, with a 4-1 victory ensuring a group win, and a quarter-final against Spain. Not only that, but Kluivert's consolation effort for the Dutch meant they edged Scotland out for second place on goal difference. Ha, ha.

The quarter-final took place on my birthday. England were fortunate to earn a penalty shootout and go through. It all added to the party atmosphere that evening, which I celebrated with a few friends. The following Wednesday evening the whole country was like a ghost town as England took on Germany in a semi-final for the second time in six years. The outcome is well documented, and prompted the question: "What's the quickest way out of Wembley?" Answer: Via the South Gate.

On the eve of the final I attended a party at the foreign press association. I'm damned if I know why I received the invitation but I took Kev along and we left with loads of freebies, as well as memories of a very dull conversation with Angus Loughran, a.k.a. Statto from BBC TV's Fantasy Football League. We had been promised that Trevor Brooking would be there – that's the only reason I went. Trev never showed, so we took the freebies and ran.

Germany won the final against the Czechs and a big cloud hung over the country. But I was pleased to be able to get back to matters West Ham, looking forward to the new season.

Gary rang me later that week to tell me a press conference was looming and to get down to Upton Park. I arrived to find a packed press lounge. Managing Director Peter Storrie walked in, together with two new signings, Mark Bowen and Florin Raducioiu. I was delighted. Not only that, Storrie announced Michael Hughes had now been signed up on a permanent contract, a free transfer, the first of its kind under the new Bosman ruling.

These were exciting times. Earlier that week, former Portuguese international and European Footballer of the Year Paulo Futre, and highly rated Southampton defender Richard Hall also joined the club. This was amazing. Having finished the previous season in a comfortable mid-table position, it seemed the club were well on the way to laying the foundations of a team that could really achieve something.

In the days when John Lyall had been manager, there may have been one or two new faces each year and a few departures, but these days it seemed wholesale changes had to occur every season. Not just in the summer months but throughout the year. Fresh blood had to be brought in on a regular basis to keep the momentum going, to placate the fans and show the club had ambition . . . and justify the massive hike in season ticket prices.

I took The Wonderful Helen to the pictures to see *Mission Impossible*. How appropriate.

With all the new signings in place I couldn't wait for the friendlies to start so we could take a look at our new talent. We won at Margate with a goal provided not by one of our new stars, but from Stevie 'Steptoe' Jones, who had rejoined the club from Bournemouth for £200,000 – amazingly, exactly the same amount as Bournemouth's VAT bill. The next day at Carshalton, a postman gave Richard Hall a delivery he won't forget in a hurry, with a tackle that was to keep him out for most of the season. I watched us win 4-0 at Dagenham & Redbridge, inspired by the silky skills of Futre. Okay, it was only Dagenham & Redbridge but we had tripped over smaller hurdles in the past, so it was pleasing to see us win so easily.

That Saturday Matt and Helen (not The Wonderful Helen, but lovely all the same) tied the knot. Kev and I decided we had better go, missing a 2-1 win at Reading with goals from Slater and Hughes. Still no sign of Foreign Florin but, we guessed, maybe Redknapp was keeping his secret weapon under wraps. Surely we didn't have another Boogers on our hands? Surely not? Florin eventually appeared in a 3-2 defeat at Torquay United and promptly received a smack in the mouth from defender Jon Gittens. Welcome to English football, Florin.

It has been documented that Florin reacted badly to such treatment and this is one of the main reasons Redknapp didn't play him when he became available again. It looked alarmingly like we were going to seriously piss off one of the best players ever to pull on a claret and blue shirt. Harry, for all his down-to-earth, laudable qualities, was not prepared to even try to handle the egos of these big foreign stars. It seemed that If they didn't do it his way, he wasn't interested. That may have been fine 10 years ago but, these days, you have to massage the egos of these guys, let them think they have the upper hand, even if they don't. Football management now is about so much more than tactics and motivation.

I travelled down to Bournemouth with Kev and met Gary and The Tortoise on the sea front mid-afternoon. Sporting my new Romania shirt, we found a convenient bar and watched the local talent. Gary piped up: "Okay, who wants a beer?" and a young fox with a very sexy French accent replied: "I do!" Gary, ever the gentleman, completely ignored her, aware that in this part of town, the local working girls would let blokes buy them a drink and then suggest something a little more pricey. Kev plucked up the courage to go and have a chat with her at the bar. She was gorgeous. A mini skirt up under her armpits and a crop top revealing a pierced belly button. I stood next to Kev so I could learn from the master. The conversation went something like this:

French tart: "What eeeeez your name?"

Kevin: "Kevin"

French tart: "You want to buy me an ooch?"

Kevin: "No"

By this time we were all falling about, as she went on to explain to Kev that her nipples were pierced as well, but she obviously couldn't get them out to show him in the bar. If he wanted to see them, he'd have to go back to her place. I think Kev was actually tempted but, if he was, he didn't let on.

We nabbed the best parking spaces at Dean Court and watched a reasonable display. 'Disco' Dale Gordon, now player-coach, was strutting his stuff for Bournemouth. Two goals from Steptoe gave us a 2-0 win and sent us back up the M3 happy. The next day Kev and I went to watch a West Ham reserve XI draw 1-

1 at Hitchin Town. There were only a handful of Hammers fans there, but locals Buzz and John, the Seller, had made the effort. Before the game, sharing a quiet pint in the bar, the telephone was ringing constantly, and an exasperated barman would answer it saying: "Yes, that's right, kick-off 3pm. Yes, that's right, it's a West Ham XI. Yes, that's right, it's just by the station. Yes, that's right, £4 adults, £2 children. Okay, thank you." We thought we were being helpful and next time the phone rang, Kev answered it himself. Of course this wasn't the only call he answered and on more than one occasion he had to lean across the bar to ask if 'Alan' was in. then the phone disappeared. Funny that.

The friendlies ended with a 4-2 defeat at my beloved Luton, a 1-0 defeat at Leyton Orient and a 4-1 win in Steve Whitton's testimonial at Colchester. The Tortoise and me queued that morning for tickets to the opening league game against Arsenal, full of that boyish, innocent enthusiasm that precedes every season. It's laughable to look back at now, but we really thought we could win.

20. Wannabe

Arsenal 2 West Ham United 0   17.8.96

After Manchester United spanked Newcastle United 5-0 in the Charity Shield, it seemed the title might be just out of reach this year. We arrived at Highbury, though, with our plastic claret and blue bowler hats sitting jauntily on the sides of our heads, fully expecting to give everyone a run for their money.

However, the team that took to the pitch for the game at Highbury was sadly reminiscent of the side that had struggled in the reserve league the season before. No Florin, no Futre, no Hall, no Dumitrescu. Instead a team that could be best described euphemistically as 'workmanlike' took to the field, the only fresh face being that of Mark Bowen, and he was only on the bench. Breacker, Rowland, Jones, Dowie, Slater and Lazaridis did not inspire me with confidence and I was right to be less than optimistic as the teams finally took to the field at 2.55pm

A 2-0 defeat was possibly the best we could have hoped for, a chance to re-group, get some injured players back and start again with two home matches in the next seven days. Rumours suggested that Futre had got the major hump because he had only been named as a substitute, and had been issued with the squad number 16, not the number 10 he was used to and felt he deserved. Whether this was true or not, he appeared on the bench for the home match against Coventry City, wearing the number 10 shirt, while John Moncur, who wore it at Arsenal, had the offer of two weeks in a luxury Portuguese villa.

West Ham were pitiful for 45 minutes, the only efforts being long-range shots from Dicksy, until Futre came on with his dodgy knees to illuminate an otherwise dull match. His running on and off the ball, his vision, passing and flicks made the extortionate amount I'd paid for my season ticket seem worthwhile already. But we could still only muster one goal, from Marc Rieper, to level the game at 1-1.

Florin finally got a start against Southampton. Whether it had been his facial injury, sustained at Torquay, that had kept him out or the fact that Harry didn't like his attitude, we may never know. Even with Florin and Futre playing, we still went behind to a Neil Heaney goal. An injury to Rieper brought Dumitrescu into the fray, as we were treated to one of the best 45 minutes of football ever seen at Upton Park. This is not an exaggeration. Although the game only ended 2-1 to West Ham, the pace and skill of our attacking players left Southampton in a spin and left us fans gasping for breath. Florin, to me, looked wonderful. Like Futre, he ran well on and off the ball and put in some excellent crosses, which Dowie, try as he might, just could not convert. Florin stood on the touchline, hands on hips, as if to say: "Hagi would have tucked that away...."

In the end the equaliser came from a cross-cum-shot by Hughes which floated over Dave Beasant and caused much debate within the media. Had he meant it, or was it a fluke? Had it been scored by David Beckham there would have been no debate, it would have been an audacious piece of skill. Personally, I think it was a fluke, but that's not the point.

Dumitrescu was tripped in the area to win us a penalty. Stupidly, he picked up the ball, shaping to take it himself, only to be manhandled out of the way by

Julian Dicks, who smashed in his first of the season to win the points and fill us with hope for two tough away trips that followed.

Successive trips to Middlesbrough and Sunderland was a little mean of the fixture computer. (I bet it isn't a computer. I bet there's some sadistic bastard who sits behind a desk at the FA trying to see how he can piss everyone off.).

Middlesbrough was a Wednesday evening and we arrived at The Riverside confident that if we played the same team that had thrashed Southampton, we would get a result.

We retired to the same pub as the previous year, hooked as we were by the paint-stripping bitter called Sheep Dip. 'Boro had also been on the spend abroad, with Ravanelli, Emerson and Juninho in their side. We built on our success against Southampton by dropping Dumi to the bench and expecting Florin and Futre to do the business up front. It was entirely possible that it could work, but it didn't. We were 3-0 down at half-time and hadn't had a sniff. Enter secret weapon Dowie, as desperation set in and Harry tried to scare Middlesbrough into submission. Hughes pulled one back with a spectacular strike but 'Boro were clearly three goals better than us on the night and it ended 4-1.

We waited in the car park with a couple of Hammers fans whose car had broken down, while they waited for the AA. The area is a little rough to say the least and we felt it best to keep them company until the cavalry arrived.

Sunday and Uncle Rupert had delivered another peach of a game – Sunderland v West Ham. I found the prospect boring, so God knows how neutrals felt about it. I hired a car for the journey, not wanting to put my decrepit Orion through a 600-mile round trip. I'd got a Renault Megane, which was smaller than I expected but

I had the most comfortable seat, so I didn't really give a toss. I had written a piece in *Hammers News Magazine* predicting a boring 0-0 draw, to teach Uncle Rupert to mess about with the schedules. After the game, Martin Tyler emerged from the press box, clutching said article. I approached him and made myself known to him, and he said he'd used the article during his Sky commentary. I smiled inwardly and decided to try out my new tape machine by interviewing a few players. I grabbed it back from Craig, who had borrowed it to interview Steve Agnew of Sunderland, and saw Florin Raducioiu standing on his todd talking on his mobile phone. I had no idea how good his English was, but approached him anyway, waving my tape machine at him. He smiled at me, assuming it was a camera, and put his arm around me to pose for the snap.

"No, no." I said. "Interview."

"Interview?"

"Words."

"Words? Ah, okay, but, er, my Eeenglish not so good."

Something told me this was going to be a struggle and just maybe I'd bitten off more than I could chew. Florin still had his arm around me, though, so I couldn't run away, which was what I really wanted to do. I talked to him for about five minutes, prompting him to give the answers I wanted, then he released me from his vice-like grip. I leapt out of the frying pan into the fire and waved my tape machine under the nose of a startled Slaven Bilic, whose English is a lot better than mine, and asked him if there was any truth in the rumours linking him with a move to Spurs. He stuttered a load of old bollocks back at me. Credit to the guy, though, he made it clear he was in this for the money and much as he loved West Ham, he had a family to consider and would move on if the right offer came in. He's a qualified lawyer, so I won't call him a wanker here.

It was a good day out really, in spite of the game. We consoled ourselves with the thought that we had stood on the terrace at Roker Park for the last time – and with double helpings of chips with curry sauce. On the way home we had a near death experience involving a lorry, the Megane's windscreen and a flying wheel nut. That put things in perspective, I can tell you.

Wimbledon came and nicked their usual three points from us at Upton Park as we looked truly awful. Futre and Dumitrescu both started but couldn't re-create the spark that had illuminated the Southampton match. Cottee came on, in an effort to try and turn the game using more orthodox methods, but all was in vain. A 2-0 defeat left West Ham in 17th place with just five points. A season that had promised much was in danger of turning into a disaster.

I missed my first, and only, game of the season when I opted to join my colleagues on our annual beano to Brighton rather than sample the delights of a Coca-Cola Cup-tie at Barnet. Despite playing third division opposition, we still struggled, and only rescued a draw with a Cottee header, a goal which turned out to be his last for West Ham.

In a way I was glad to have missed the game. It had sounded pretty dire but, on the other hand, it was the first game I'd missed for nearly a year and, at the time, sad things like that were important to me.

I soon got back in the swing, though. A trip to Nottingham Forest is always a pleasure, particularly when you have lunch with the lovely Christina before the game, she drops you outside the away entrance and your team wins 2-0. We felt like we had won at Old Trafford. A win of any description was rare, even this early in the season, but an away win was extra special, particularly as Rieper had been sent off while the score was still delicately poised at 1-0. Bowen scored a very rare goal and Hughes the other. Lazaridis had the game of his life and ran the show. I was pleased for him, as he had overcome a serious injury to win back a place in the starting line up. A very genial guy, Gary interviewed him after the game and had trouble shutting him up. I grabbed a quick word with Rieper, who hadn't been happy at the sending off and seemed likely to appeal.

Four days later Barnet were beaten unconvincingly, 1-0, with a header from Bilic. He was starting to piss me off with his attitude. I sold my Croatia shirt in a defiant gesture and a few days later flogged my Romania shirt, too. I felt I had been short changed.

21. Breakfast At Tiffanys

West Ham United 4 Nottingham Forest 1 23.10.96

September ended with another defeat, at the hands of Liverpool. It was frightening to see the way Stan Collymore outpaced Rieper to slide home the first – if only Alvin had still been around. Bilic equalised with his second in two games but Michael Thomas grabbed a second half winner.

It was clear that despite all the investment made in the team over the summer we were still lacking a cutting edge. The only goal scored so far by a recognised striker had been Cottee's effort at Barnet. However, I couldn't help thinking we were digging our own grave to an extent, by leaving players of the calibre of Florin and Dumi on the bench. The scrap for points in the Premiership is a fierce one and we didn't have time to experiment and mess about. We needed action, fast. Harry signed the Portugeezer Hugo Porfirio on loan from Sporting Lisbon, the side that had crushed us 5-1 at home in our centenary match at the end of last season. He came on against Liverpool and looked a useful acquisition but we lacked the firepower up front to convert the chances he could potentially create.

I left Upton Park that afternoon with a cloud over my head. My only consolation was that Collymore had copped a cup of Coke on the bonce after scoring. Whoever threw that should play cricket for England.

A lengthy gap for internationals meant our first game of October would not take place until the 12th. I took the opportunity to watch QPR v Port Vale with Stuart, the QPR fan, a match Vale won 2-1. It made me feel a little better. We might be losing too, but at least we were losing to the Liverpools of this world. It also brought home the stark reality of our predicament. A few years back, QPR were turning us over in the Premiership. The fall from grace could be swift and, if not careful, permanent.

We decided to make a weekend of it for the Everton game. I met Kev, Matt, Helen and Buzz on the Friday night, eagerly anticipating the game with an optimism that was almost pathetic in its innocence. Buzz was kipping at Matt's and on arriving home they attacked a bottle of brandy before starting to write an article for OLAS. Helen came down at four in the morning to find Matt slumped at the keyboard, his chin pressing down the space bar, and an article apparently 1,000 pages long. The article was, in fact, one page long, with 999 blank pages after it. Matt showed it to me when we turned up at his flat. It was entitled 'Poke it, large!' and was the funniest thing I had ever read.

Unfortunately it had nothing to do with West Ham, so it never made OLAS.

Relieved of driving duties for the day, I took advantage on reaching The Stanley, the pub opposite Goodison Park, and picked up where I had left off the night before. By the time kick-off arrived I was a little worried that the over-vigilant policing might prevent me entering the stadium, on account of the fact I couldn't walk in a straight line, while my breath could have opened a bank vault. Kev and I were holding each other up as we took our seats. I really don't know why we travelled all that way to miss most of the game in a drunken haze. All I remember is we lost 2-1, Hugo tore them apart but we had no one to stick the chances away.

We stopped at Helen's parents on the way home to be fed sandwiches and, you guessed it, beer. Not a good day for West Ham. And an awful day for my liver.

We faced three home matches in a row and if our season was to progress in anything like a meaningful fashion, we needed something from all of them. This was optimistic, as previous form had not suggested a win of any description would be forthcoming, but with one of them a cup-tie under lights, anything could happen. The third was a clash with rock bottom Blackburn Rovers, so maybe optimism was not misplaced.

The most difficult of the three appeared to be the first game, the visit of Leicester City. Now managed by Martin O'Neill and much better organised than on their previous visit in the Premiership, we edged past them 1-0 with a Moncur goal engineered by the irrepressible Hugo.

I had been on a prospective sales manager's course at Gatwick and a few of my colleagues were Chelsea fans. On the Wednesday morning we woke up to the news that Matthew Harding, the Chelsea director, had been killed in a helicopter crash while coming back from their Coca-Cola Cup tie at Bolton. There were some glum faces around that day, mine included. Say what you like about Chelsea, or about the majority of the twats that follow them, Matthew Harding was just a fan, albeit a fan with bundles of cash.

That night, West Ham turned on one of those cup performances against Nottingham Forest that used to be the norm, but now seem so rare. Hugo was the star of the show, setting up Dowie for his first goal of the season and then setting up his last of the season, sandwiching a token effort from Colin Cooper. Dowie then returned the favour with a deft back-heel for Hugo to get the third, while Haaland fouled Lazaridis to concede a penalty for the fourth. I had thought Dowie might take it to collect his hat-trick – after all, he normally takes them for Northern Ireland. No chance. Dicksy hammered home the fourth from the spot and I was pleased the players did not allow sentiment to get in the way and let a player take a penalty just because he was on a hat-trick. How unprofessional would that be?

The chance to make it three in a row came the following Saturday, with the Rovers game. Before the match I had an hour-long photo shoot for the front cover of the second edition of *Irrational*. I had been told to comb my hair for once, and turn up wearing a West Ham shirt, and there would be a 'model' waiting for me. I wasn't sure whether to expect Caprice or an Airfix kit but was pleasantly surprised when I clapped eyes on Lesley, wearing thigh-high 'shag-me' boots and a tasty little black number. Lesley was one of the *Hammers News Magazine* sellers, a lovely lass from Glasgow. I had a little trouble understanding her but she really entered into the spirit of things and cameraman Richard Austin exhausted several rolls of film. Two little kids asked Lesley if she was 'Tiffany' from Eastenders. "Och aye, I am that!" she replied and kissed them both on the cheek. They went away, impressed at what a nice girl she was and the fact she must have been a great actress to do such a good cockney accent.

The photos from the shoot came back from the chemist's on time, and made the second edition as big a success as the first. The picture of Lesley sitting on my knee on the front cover was the main talking point for most people. And for those of you who never got the chance to ask me, no I don't know if she was wearing any.

My modelling career back on ice, I took my seat for an entertaining game that saw West Ham come from a goal down to win 2-1. Dowie set up Hugo for the equaliser and Henning Berg, who had scored their first half goal, secured the three points for us with a spectacular diving header of an own goal. I laughed. You wouldn't catch one of our players scoring such a brilliant own goal.

Blackburn Rovers were in a spot of bother. They had sold Alan Shearer to Newcastle for £15m and had not adequately replaced him. Dalglish and Harford had both moved on and, not for the first time nor the last, caretaker Tony Parkes was in charge. The funny thing about Tony Parkes is, he really does look like a caretaker. The other funny thing about Blackburn was they had just signed a major sponsorship deal with my company, CIS. The ink hadn't so much as dried when Shearer was heading for Newcastle and a team that two years hence had won the Premiership, was staring down the barrel of the relegation gun.

The good run came to an end at Tottenham, where Chris Armstrong scored the winner after a Bilic cock-up so blatant we felt he may be trying to endear himself to his prospective new employers. He tried to make up for it by hitting the post with a minute to go. And Hugo could have had a hat-trick but he didn't, so we lost.

I hired a car again for the drive to Newcastle. This time I made sure it would be a bit more comfortable, a Honda Accord with CD player and air conditioning. Very nice. Even so, at 5am that morning I had to question my sanity as I sat waiting for the frost to clear from the windscreen. Gary phoned me on my mobile: "Can you believe we are doing this? Five in the bloody morning?" I had to agree it was ridiculous but, like everything else, it seemed like a good idea at the time. Our companions for the day were to be Craig, Kev and The Tortoise. We arrived early enough to spend some meaningful time in the Strawberry, where The Tortoise overdosed on lettuce and nearly got our heads kicked in. I dragged him off to try and sober him up while Kev and Craig went to a nearby pub advertising lunchtime 'adult' entertainment. By the time Kev joined me inside the stadium he had a smile on his face the width of the A1. Someone had a good time.

West Ham started brightly, with Florin running his nuts off. A headed goal from Keith Rowland was a rarity. Well, it was his only one, ever, that's how rare. We hung on for long enough to suggest a win might actually be a possibility but Peter Beardsley spoiled the party near the end with an equaliser. By 90 minutes we were happy to hold out for a draw we had hardly expected, but fully deserved. If a Keith Rowland goal was rare, a trip to the Metro shopping centre yielded something even rarer. Three Buzz Lightyear figures. The kids would have a good Christmas. We pressed the middle button on his chest and he summed up our day: "To infinity and beyond!"

22. What's Love Got To Do With It?

Sheffield Wed. 0 West Ham United 0   30.12.96

I asked Lucy if Kev and me could come up and spend the weekend in Sheffield while we took in the game. Not only did she agree, she asked me to get seven tickets so that she and several members of her friends and family could also attend and meet the famous OLAS crew (something like that, anyway)

Meanwhile I received a phone call from a Canadian television producer by the name of David Hall, who was shooting a series of short films about the English and their way of life. Called *Café Utopia*, one of these films was to be about the English obsession with football and having read my book, he wanted to centre the documentary around my fascination with West Ham. He cleared it with the authorities at West Ham to use the Boleyn Ground to make the film before and during the Derby County match and I arrived at reception at noon, with Kev for moral support.

We both achieved boyhood ambitions, walking up the players' tunnel into the crisp November air, pretending it was a full house and we were about to make our debuts. Instead all we got was a ticking off from the groundsman for treading on the pitch. David and his co-producer wife, Annie, interviewed us for an hour or so, then followed us down to the Millers Well, where they interviewed Matt and Helen, and Simon, a soldier who had written to me from Bosnia to tell me how much he had enjoyed the book. I had invited him to join us for a drink before I knew about the TV crew, so he got a whole lot more than he bargained for.

If you think the TV life is glamorous, think again. We stood for two hours in the freezing cold being interviewed, having to repeat virtually every answer because someone was shouting, or a trolley went past, and there's always some helpful berk trying to get in on the act. It was fun, as they say, but I wouldn't want to do it for a living.

They had me miked up for the match itself, which ended in a 1-1 draw. Bishop scored with what he later admitted to be a fluky shot from outside the box but Dean Sturridge equalised just before half-time and neither side had the wit or guile to grab a winner. After the game, Dave and Annie stuck faithfully by our sides and recorded our verdicts. We never did see the final tape. Maybe they were just winding us up.

Midweek, we faced Second Division Stockport County at Upton Park in the fourth round of the Coca-Cola Cup. A formality on paper but we are talking about West Ham. Florin got a start and put us ahead with his first-ever goal for the club. But the writing was on the wall soon after the second half began, when a defensive slip by Dicksy allowed Stockport to equalise. We looked limp and lifeless and hadn't deserved to win the game.

Still, we were still in the competition and we put it to the back of our minds on arrival in Sheffield in my new Mondeo. We were treated to tea and sarnies at Lucy's house. Her dad, Ian the Professor, was to join us at the match, together with some of her friends, keen to sample the big match atmosphere. Well, never mind, Wednesday v West Ham is better than nothing. Lucy's friend, Nikki, arrived and we went off to the pub, arranging to meet the others at the tram stop by the university.

I took a bit of a shine to Nikki, who was a nurse, and

just had the most wicked smile. We got along really well and as Kev stopped to withdraw some cash at the tram stop, he said to me: "You're in there, mate." I told him not to be stupid but as the day progressed I found the chemistry between us growing. Ian, the Professor, is a Stoke City fan in real life and as I sat next to him watching the game he reminisced about the days of Dobing, Ritchie and Conroy.

Kev was late taking his seat, having been nabbed by Gary to do a radio interview with Shelley Webb on the merits of foreigners in the English game. She had wanted to speak to Gary, a fanzine editor, 15 minutes before kick-off. What did she think he would be doing? Sitting around twiddling his thumbs? She got more that she bargained for as a very drunk Kev professed his undying love for Ilie Dumitrescu to the listening world. The game was a huge waste of time, Hughes having our best effort in a 0-0 draw. The Professor and wife, Wendy, left town, leaving me, Lucy, Kev and Nikki to our own devices in the house, via several pubs on the way back from Hillsborough.

We found the music room and Kev and I had a quick jam session, playing hits from Oasis on keyboard and guitar. We had all planned to go out that evening, to a club in town called The Roundhouse. It was a while before we were due to leave and we had run out of beer, so I volunteered to walk to the off-licence. Nikki offered to come with me and explained how she had recently split up with her long-term boyfriend and that she wasn't looking for a relationship at the moment. I took this as a 'keep yer grubby mitts off me' kind of talk but, later in the pub, she was all over me, rubbing herself deliberately against me and forcing me to think of 0-0 draws to save my sanity. In the cab on the way to the club, she grabbed my hand and was staring into my eyes so deeply it was almost embarrassing. I dismissed it as the drink talking but when we danced on an almost deserted dance floor, she kissed me and the electricity flowed through me. Wow! I thought.

I should have smelled a rat there and then, as a group of blokes turned up and I could hear in the background the sound of knives being sharpened. Nikki disappeared for a while and came back in tears. Lucy had a tear-up with someone and left. Kev, feeling unwell, hadn't come with us. He'd stayed at the house, so I was left in a strange club, in a strange city, with a strange woman.

I dragged her outside at midnight and hailed a cab. I couldn't get any sense out of her, we were both a bit drunk, and having whetted my appetite, all I really wanted was another snog.

When we got back to Lucy's she grabbed my hand and led me upstairs to her room, locked the door behind us and shagged my brains out. Wow! I thought, not for the first time that day. And it wasn't the last either. In fact, we got no sleep at all, the only time that has ever happened to me. I drove back home with Kev at Sunday lunchtime on diesel fuel and adrenaline. Kev said nothing except: "Told you so."

The lack of goals continued at home to Aston Villa the following Wednesday. We just could not put the ball in the net. We had scored a meagre 13 league goals all season not one of them from a recognised striker. Dicks, Bowen, Bilic, Hughes, Moncur, Porfirio and even Keith Rowland had scored. But Dowie and Raducioiu, the two "strikers" in the truest sense of the world, had only managed three between them, and they had all come in the cup.

Tony Cottee had signed for Malaysian club Selangor for £775,000 but was still training with the club until their season began in the New Year. I watched a training session with tears in my eyes, realising that the soon to depart TC was the only player out there who seemed to know where the goal was.

We lost 2-0 to Villa and were 2-0 down to Manchester United the following Sunday. But this was United in front of the live cameras and we always pull out something a bit special. Dowie was playing his heart out, bless him, while Dumitrescu was having the game of his life. We were unlucky to be two behind but, at last, Harry showed some faith in Florin. On as a substitute for only a few minutes, he showed his defender a clean pair of heels, cut inside from the left and curled a perfect shot past Schmeichel and inside the far post. Two minutes later, clean through, Michael Hughes was tripped by Rudolph, the red nosed reindeer, who had clearly turned up a few weeks early.

Julian's penalty was hit with such ferocity that if Schmeichel had got a hand to it, he would have been nursing four broken fingers. The excitement of that 90 minutes disguised the fact that we were in big trouble, still gazing up at too many teams above us at far too late a stage of the season.

That week I took the opportunity to see the youth team in action, at Colchester in an FA Youth Cup tie. The kids won 3-1 and looked to be more than capable of repeating the performance of the previous season.

I returned to Sheffield for a party at Lucy's, to be told the whole episode with naughty nurse Nikki was a huge mistake. Not only that, it was *my* fault. Well of course it was my fault; I am a bloke, after all.

23. Un-Break My Heart

Stockport County 2 West Ham United 1 18.12.96

Matt volunteered to drive to Stockport and we got under way via various stops in Hertfordshire to pick up Buzz and his mate Paul. In the obligatory traffic jam on the M6, it started to rain. Nothing serious at this point, nothing more than a shower, we thought. Stockport, being a suburb of Manchester, was bound to be experiencing some rain. But this rain was persistent, it was freezing and it was painful.

We parked the car and went to find a pub, although with little time to spare. Inside, we found The Tortoise, doing his best to get his head kicked in by opening his gob in pissed mode. We turned up just in time to save his neck. It might sound like sour grapes now but I'm convinced that had the game not been scheduled for live transmission by Uncle Rupert, it would have been cancelled. The referee inspected the pitch and deemed the it 'playable' when, to quote Danny Baker, Moses might have deemed it 'partable.' No sign of Florin again, Harry claiming that he'd gone shopping at Harvey Nicks with his in-laws rather than face a trip to a rain-soaked Stockport.

It was inevitable we would lose. There had been little doubt of that from the moment the referee put the whistle to his lips in the 90th minute of the first match. But the manner of our exit, the feeble way we conceded a first half lead, and the astonishing nature of Dowie's own goal, just went to prove that even the most cynical of West Ham fans can't always predict how bad things can get.

Standing on open terrace, my new suede jacket ruined, we trudged, dejected back to the car, having rescued Kev from the pitch, in an attempt not to get at the Stockport fans, but to give our own players a good kicking.

Matt's decision to avoid the M6 by driving us down Snake Pass at breakneck speed did nothing to improve my mood. It's hard to be a West Ham fan at the best of times. On nights like this, you just wish you had been born in America, or Africa, or anywhere where the name West Ham United has never been heard.

One more morale-sapping defeat came before Christmas, at the hands of Chelsea at Stamford Bridge. Hugo had pulled us level before Zola turned Dicksy inside out and upside down to restore their lead. The game ended 3-1 but at least we hadn't expected anything from it. I'll never forget the hacks in the press box slating Julian and talking in pidgin Italian. Tossers.

The OLAS Christmas party was a subdued and understated affair. Suffering from an injury list longer than the Hammers' first team squad, we were without Gary and Kev due to illness. Buzz was taking it very seriously, though, downing double tequila and pineapple juices but that might have just been to kill the pain of being a West Ham supporter in December 1996. Bill Drury joined us for a swift half, as did Gjermund Holte, editor of *Scandinavian Bubbles*, over for the Christmas games. We headed off to the chinky next door and then on to The Tortoise's straw box, hoping we might wake up the next morning and find it had all been a terrible dream.

It was, in fact, a very real nightmare. I was almost pleased that the Boxing Day game against Wimbledon was called off at short notice – we would almost certainly have lost if the game had gone ahead. Kev had made arrangements for his sister to drop him at my house so I could drive to the game, but I only checked Ceefax after he'd arrived to find the game was off. Instead of a visit to Selhurst Park, I had a trip to Turnpike Lane to take Kev home.

Sunderland offered the final opposition of the year. Actually they offered no opposition at all; they were the only side not to look dangerous going forward at Upton Park all season (apart from West Ham, of course). Bilic scored his third of the campaign and Williamson hit the post when it looked easier to score. Despite Sunderland's lack of potency, we were painfully aware that one goal may not be enough. With two minutes to go, the crowd's urgent calls for Florin to be thrown into the action were answered by Frank Lampard, standing in for a bed-ridden flu victim Harry. I could see the management's thought process. "We'll bung him on with two minutes to go, then they can't say we didn't give him a chance, and he wont aggravate the situation by scoring..."

But score he did. Turning his marker on the half-way line, Florin raced through to beat Perez with consummate ease, flicking a metaphoric 'V' sign at the bench and sharing a cheeky 'thanks for your support, guys' type of grin with the Bobby Moore Lower. I felt sure that we had been instrumental in engineering a goal.

Unfortunately, we could not be instrumental in persuading Florin to stay.

24. Quit Playing Games

West Ham United 0 Wrexham 1 25.1.1997

New Year's Day and I suppose I should have been grateful we didn't have a trek to the other end of the country to be beaten in a terrible game of football. Instead we were beaten in a terrible game of football at Upton Park, by a Nottingham Forest side doomed to relegation and so desperate they had turned to Stuart Pearce for managerial inspiration. Kevin Campbell scored his first goal since his opening day hat-trick against Coventry City, which said everything.

The third round of the FA Cup saw me back on familiar territory, away at Wrexham, home-town of my ex-fiancée. The fact we had drawn Wrexham inspired me to get in touch with her again. I knew she was still lecturing at East London Polytechnic, so I left a message for her there and, to my surprise, she called me back.

It must have been a good four years since I had spoken to her. All the good things about our relationship came flooding back to me as we chatted on the phone, so I arranged to go over for dinner the following week. I didn't have reconciliation on my mind, just a chance to repair a few fences and maybe rescue a friendship.

The locals in Wrexham were far from friendly, barring us from virtually every pub near the ground. My local knowledge helped, though, and I found us a pub, albeit packed to the rafters, where we could have a quiet pint. The Tortoise had driven us to the game in his clapped out Escort, reminiscent in many ways of my old Orion, but it did us proud and got us there in plenty of time. Not before we had skated around on a few roads, thinking the clutch had gone, only to realise lack of grip on icy roads was the problem. Kev had balanced his can of beer on the roof while looking at the car – and left it there by mistake. It only fell off three miles later, having frozen itself to the body work.

We peeked through a gap in the gates to find the pitch covered in snow. We felt sure the game would be postponed once kick-off time approached and the referee realised the ground was bone hard.

To our astonishment, the tie went ahead, the groundsman digging out the blue line marker and the orange ball. Poor Hugo Porfirio, having never seen snow in his life, must have wondered what planet he was on. It obviously didn't affect him too much, as he curled a precise equaliser into the top corner from 25 yards out to square a game which really shouldn't have gone ahead in the first place.

We signed Mike Newell on loan in a bid to boost our lack of strikers but it became very apparent, very soon, that it was Newell by name, Newell Post by nature. He was not going to be the answer. Well, not unless the question was: "Can we find a donkey to play up front?" If that was the question, he was definitely the answer. I've seen houses move quicker than Newell.

Despite his obvious lack of ability, or perhaps because of it, he was selected for the team to play at Anfield. We all drew in deep breaths and covered our eyes. You know what this game is like, though. When we should get murdered, we pull off a result; when we should cruise, we get mullered. We got a 0-0 draw at Anfield, against a Liverpool team within touching distance of the title and still harbouring hopes of progress in the Cup Winners' Cup. In fact we were unlucky not to win, Rieper and Steptoe both squandering good chances.

In midweek, our chance for revenge against Wrexham was foiled by the weather. An unusual one this time, as fog had shrouded Upton Park all day, but nonetheless the game wasn't called off until I had already arrived.

Quite why Uncle Rupert picked our home match against Leeds United for their Monday Night Special is also a mystery. The game was effectively over the minute Leeds scored. Discontent among the fans manifested itself in the form of a red card campaign, aimed at persuading the Board to at least open talks with a character named Michael Tabor, an entrepreneur racehorse owner and alleged West Ham fan, who apparently was willing to let the club have access to some of his reported £30m fortune.

Now obviously a man with that sort of money isn't going to hand over dosh without some sort of deal being in place, but it appeared that the Hammers Board weren't even prepared to talk to the guy. It was this that so angered everyone into protests reminiscent of the bond scheme in 1991-92.

That winter of discontent ended in relegation. When Leeds scored a second and condemned us to another defeat, I could only see the same outcome for us this time too. Five league wins all season was worse than at the same stage in 1991-92, so it's hardly surprising that when Wrexham finally got to play us, on the Saturday afternoon reserved for the fourth round, they scored an 89th minute winner.

Fans poured onto the pitch in protest. What more could we do? We had written all there was to write, we had spoken to all the people there were to talk to, and direct action was all that was left. Something the team at that time wouldn't recognise if it bit them on the arse.

25. Where Do You Go?

West Ham United 4 Tottenham Hotspur 3 24.2.97

It wasn't difficult to predict that Arsenal would beat us. Morale was on the floor and despite Matthew Rose doing his best by scoring an own goal for us (that bloke 'O.G.' was ominously close to the top of our scorers' list again), we couldn't hold on for so much as a point. We showed our red cards and voiced our protest. Whether it did any good or not, we can only speculate. But some transfer money miraculously appeared from somewhere.

Maybe the directors had been looking down the back of their sofas and found £2.3m in loose change to buy Paul Kitson from Newcastle United. Wherever they found it from, they must have found some more, as John Hartson was also signed from Arsenal in a deal worth a staggering £3.2m. It's never been fully explained, to me anyway, where this money came from. I'm not particularly bothered but I would like to know if the directors re-mortgaged the stadium, just in case interest rates start rising.

Before the signing of the dynamic duo, the formality of a defeat at Ewood Park had to be observed. Only 2-1 this time, which may have been seen as an improvement in some eyes but, in mine, was still the result of shambolic defending, coupled with inept forward play. Poor Les Sealey, making only his second appearance in goal for West Ham, found himself on the losing side again. Rio Ferdinand came on as a substitute and scored to provide the only highlight in another miserable away day performance.

Several names had been mentioned to bolster the West Ham attack before the signing of John and Paul. Wimbledon's Dean Holdsworth was a serious possibility, Duane Darby of Hull City, one of the more hilarious. Although unsure of the wisdom of forking out so much cash for two reserve team players, I was willing to give them the benefit of the doubt as I travelled up the M1 to Derby to watch both players make their West Ham debuts.

The new Mondeo was also making its debut, as we sat in a traffic jam on the M1 and a Manchester City fan gave it the large one as he sailed past. Within seconds he was stopping for the traffic, too, and The Tortoise leapt out of the car, waddled down the motorway and tapped on our sky blue friend's window. The guy shit himself, which was all Darren had wanted to achieve, before running back to a round of applause.

The old Baseball Ground in Derby is in the middle of an industrial estate, which itself is sited in the middle of nowhere. This must have been in their thinking when they found the site for Pride Park, because it suffers from exactly the same problems. As at most clubs, away fans are tucked into the least convenient part of the ground, with the worst view and usually with the low, winter sun in their eyes. I'm not complaining. I wish West Ham would do it, instead of giving away fans the luxury of the lower tier of the Centenary Stand. It's just the way it is.

We took to the field against Derby County with high hopes of a revival. Instead, within 15 minutes, Hartson had been booked for a challenge on Igor Stimac, which would see him suspended for two games. Terrific. Nothing seemed to have changed. We still looked hopeless in defence, midfield and attack. Apart from that we were okay. Asanovic scored from the spot and

Derby didn't have to play all that well to hang on.

Kitson was getting the bird from the Derby fans and it seemed to be getting to him, as he carefully directed a double-barrelled dustman's blow in their direction – the only thing he aimed accurately all afternoon.

I was depressed. We had spent a ton of cash and appeared to be no better off in the ability department. Relegation seemed a certainty. 13 defeats from 25 games – only five wins all season – made sickening reading. Despite our big money investments, it was hard to see where the next goal was coming from.

I had been receiving a lot of 'fan mail', for want of a better expression, as a result of the book. This surprised and delighted me, as in my experience people only wrote to you if they wanted to complain. I did get one critical letter, complaining that I was a part-timer because I missed the games at Highbury and White Hart Lane in 1993-94. Fair enough.

The majority of the letters were very nice. I even received complimentary ones from Luton fans. I wrote back to everyone and some kept the correspondence going. Being a sucker for a good letter, I kept it going too. Brita wrote to me from Welsh Wales. She's not Welsh, though, having been born in London and is half-Finnish. It's a long story. Simon, the serving soldier in Bosnia, had written in and had met us before the home game against Derby County. I also received letters from the USA, Canada, Holland and, after the Derby game, Norway. Steve Blowers, from *Hammers News Magazine*, handed me a couple of letters. The first was from a sports psychologist by the name of Dr George Sik (pronounced shick, in case you were worried). He had been holding a course in Luton, of all places, bought the book to pass the long hotel-bound evenings and had thoroughly enjoyed it. A Newcastle United fan, we kept our correspondence going.

The second letter was from Birgit, a TV weathergirl from Norway. Now I know what you are thinking – and yes, I thought it was a wind up too. The letter, very funny and witty, went on for ages. There was an address at the top, so I thought it only polite to respond. I sent the letter off and thought no more about it. Within days a reply landed on my doormat and the start of a very intense correspondence began.

Brita, from Wales, came down to meet me and the OLAS gang for the home match against Newcastle United. Torrential rain in London, and the fact the game was not being shown by Uncle Rupert, meant it was called off, and we would have to wait for a glimpse of the new dynamic duo at home. Brita had a wasted journey.

A big fan of Julian Dicks, Brita had asked if I could arrange a meeting. I had indicated that there was always ample opportunity down at the training ground to get access to your favourite players but I sensed she wanted something a little more intimate. I contacted Kirk Blows, editor of *Hammers News* at the time, for which I was a regular contributor. He put me in touch with Dicksy's agent, Rachel Anderson, who told me to meet her in reception after the Newcastle game, whenever it should occur, and she would see what she could do. Sorted.

Hartson and Kitson finally made their home debuts in the home match with Tottenham Hotspur on February 24. Similar weather conditions prevailed, with a swirling wind mixed in, but this was going out on TV, so the show had to go on. Sheringham gave Spurs an early lead and we all held our heads, yet the team appeared to be playing well, with Dicks and Hughes making progress down the flanks. Julian headed an equaliser and Hughes went close before Upton Park erupted at the sight of Paul Kitson opening his account, stooping to guide a wind-assisted corner into the net past a hapless Ian

Walker.

Anderton equalised with a shot which was going well wide before the wind blew it inside the post, then Hartson wrapped his head around a cross from Dicksy to make it 3-2. Hartson ran to the Chicken Run to receive his applause, kissing the badge. Kitson followed closely behind him. Maybe we had found a couple of decent strikers after all? Whether we had or not, the defensive frailties were still apparent, as David Howells was given acres of space to equalise from the edge of the box.

Hartson made a nuisance of himself and forced the penalty, which won the game. Dicks again hitting it home with such ferocity we feared for the safety of the crowd behind the goal. This time there was no comeback for Spurs, and we won a thrilling and morale-boosting match 4-3. Our first win of 1997, it was also the first time we had scored more than two goals in a league match all season.

There was light at the end of the tunnel.

26. Isn't It A Wonder

West Ham United 3 Chelsea 2 12.3.97

The light at the end of the tunnel proved to be nothing
more than a train coming the other way. At least that's
the way it seemed as we slumped to defeat at Elland
Road, Lee Sharpe scoring for once. Buzz and his
Hertfordshire gang hit the pub early and were having
such a good time they decided not to let a stupid game
of football ruin their day, so they stayed there. Sensible
people.

Another windy day, with crisp packets and carrier
bags swirling around on the pitch along with the other
22 pieces of rubbish that were floating around on it. This
was not a good game. Michael Hughes wasn't enjoying
himself and decided to take an early bath. I wished I
could have done the same. Instead we had to hurtle
back down the motorway in The Tortoise's Escort,
narrowly avoiding death as his rear nearside tyre blew
out in the fast lane at 80mph. I was sitting in the back
and watched the sparks flying out the back of the car.
My main concern was not that we would be hit, but that
we would blow up. The calmest people in the car were
Darren himself, who guided the car safely to the hard
shoulder, and Gary, who wound down the window to
warn traffic approaching from behind.

On the hard shoulder, counting our blessings, we
emptied the boot to get out the spare tyre. Fortunately
there was one, but the wheel jack had rusted solid and
couldn't be moved. Me, Darren and Dave attempted to

lift the corner of the car while Gary changed the wheel but it just wasn't going to happen. Ford Escorts are heavy little beasts. Eventually we realised that if he could lift it long enough to just wedge the jack in position, rusted or not, it would support the car long enough to change the wheel. We motored on, gingerly, nursing aching arms and trying hard not to drag our knuckles along the ground. Gary celebrated our survival by opening a bottle of red wine and producing four glasses. Extraordinary man.

We were nursing aching hearts, too. Hartson had missed the defeat at Leeds through suspension and would also miss the visit of Chelsea. With Kitson and Dowie up front, and Hugo restored to the wing, we more than matched Chelsea for the majority of the first half, until a wayward pass from Bishop was intercepted by Zola, who squared for the unmarked Vialli to open the scoring. A real Italian Job.

A half-time chat obviously worked wonders, as Hugo wriggled his way into the box and was hauled over for a penalty. Dicksy's unerring spot kick brought us level. Minutes later Kitson raced onto a through ball and smashed it home with obvious delight. With a few minutes to go victory seemed assured but Mark Hughes equalised and the stands emptied faster than my bank account at the start of the month.

The game seemed destined to be a draw until, with just seconds left, a corner from the left was met by Dowie's head and Kitson steered it in for his second of the night. In the space of three games he had become joint second top scorer with three, behind Julian with six, five of which were spot kicks. 'Nuff said.

We then faced three tough away trips in a row. We travelled to Villa Park secure in the knowledge we had come away unbeaten in our last two visits. We made that three with a tepid 0-0 draw. The promising Frank

Lampard, however, who was becoming a regular in the side, broke his leg and would miss the rest of the season.

Before the trip to Wimbledon I made my first TV appearance, on the cable channel Granada Talk. The show was hosted by Jeremy Nicholas, now the matchday announcer at Upton Park, and my role was to challenge Ray Spiller, aka 'The Statmaster', on his knowledge of West Ham in the 1985-86 season.

We were asked five questions each, after which it was 5-5. At that point we were both allowed to ask a question of our own, which neither of us got, so it went to sudden death. Ray barked out the answer before me, so his unbeaten record remained intact. I left happy knowing I had pushed him further than anyone had done before. I was invited back for another crack at a later date and happily accepted.

At Selhurst Park, I took up my seat to find Barney, my old mate from school who I travelled to football with in the 80s, sitting behind me. We spent most of the game reminiscing and missed most of the action. Wimbledon went ahead but West Ham were a different proposition these days and, after riding a bit of luck, including a missed penalty by Vinny Jones, Stan Lazaridis popped up with an equaliser that kept the travelling faithful happy.

Birgit continued to write letters the length of small novels, to which I would write equally long replies. She made arrangements to come over in April for a few days, and I invited her to stay with me in Bexley rather than fork out for a hotel. George was also writing regularly and was egging me on to join him at Scribes, Terry Venables' wine bar in Kensington, for a night out. Several letters and phone calls later, I made arrangements to meet on the weekend Birgit was over, so she could enjoy the delights of Scribes too and, who knows, maybe meet a few proper players.

The third away game of the trio was at Highfield Road. Coventry City were fellow strugglers and the game took top billing on *Match of the Day* as the proverbial 'six-pointer'. Marc Rieper continued his habit of scoring in matches involving Coventry. Unfortunately, this one was at the wrong end to put Coventry 1-0 up. It was one of the best atmospheres I had experienced at an away match. The recent signings, plus form of one defeat in five, bred a new confidence among the fans as well as the players. Hartson scored a brilliant equaliser and within minutes Rio put us 2-1 ahead, celebrating large style in front of us. Suddenly the Coventry fans were not so cocky.

Hartson wrapped up the points with a third in the second half and it seemed there would be a race between him and Kitson to see who could score the most by the end of the season. I had to pinch myself. Transfer deadline day arrived, yielding another new signing. Steve Lomas, a combative midfielder and Northern Ireland international, arrived from Manchester City in a £1.6m move. The Board must have found another sofa, I thought, as I tore up my red card and tossed it in the bin.

Mark Bowen and Steve Mautone moved on but didn't re-coup anything like the sort of money that was being spent. Instead of chanting *Where's The Money Gone?*, we were chanting *Where's The Money From?* Never satisfied, I know, but we had gone from one extreme to the other and I was concerned that this tremendous outlay might be damaging for the future of the club. Our short term future, at least, looked secure but there were to be a few more scares along the way in a season that held our interest to the very end.

27. I Believe I Can Fly

West Ham United 2 Everton 2 19.4.97

Lomas made his debut in the home game with Middlesbrough, along with Richard Hall, who had finally shaken off his injury picked up in pre-season at Carshalton. Hall was effectively a new signing, our first chance to get a look at him. The game ended 0-0, which was a disappointment. We were getting greedy. Six weeks ago we would have killed for a goalless draw. Now we expected to score three a game.

Lomas looked tigerish, a good tackler with the added secret weapon of a humongous throw. It was hard to see why City had let him go. Just when things were rolling along nicely, Southampton threw a spanner in the works by beating us at The Dell and making us look like the pile of cack we had been in January. In truth, Southampton were pretty dire too, but they had some good players, including the on-loan Eyal Berkovic, who scored the second after Jim Magilton had missed a penalty for them and Jason Dodd had been sent off. Defeat was comprehensive and left us staring down the barrel again.

Meanwhile I was also staring down the barrel, facing the wrath of Kev, Matt and Helen, who had asked me to sort out tickets for the last game of the season, away at Old Trafford.

After Bondholders, first refusal was being offered to season ticket holders who could produce ticket stubs from the Stockport County match on December 18. Kev, Matt and Helen had given me their tickets to 'look after' and I had, well, you know, kind of mislaid them. Okay, I lost them. I searched high and low and on reflection, I wondered if maybe they had got so wet that night on the Edgeley Park terrace they had simply disintegrated.

I engaged in a lengthy dialogue with the ticket office. Quoting Matt's credit card details and providing copies of the match programme and a fanzine I had bought at Stockport to prove I had been there. I got on bended knees in front of Steve Kitcher, the ticket office manager, pleading with him, saying that if I didn't get tickets for the final game, Matt, Helen and Kev would put my head on a spike on London Bridge. Steve could make no promises. I waited anxiously.

Kitson and Hartson were, to my mind, the David Cross and Paul Goddard of the 90s. Hartson was strong and powerful, a good header of the ball, and worthy of the mantle of 'Psycho,' although it was never levelled at him. Kitson, on the other hand, though not particularly pacy, was very intelligent, had quick feet and a very accurate shot under pressure. While many players over the years at West Ham possessed these qualities, few of them gelled the way Hartson and Kitson had done. I looked forward confidently to the home game against Everton and the away match at Leicester City, predicting four points, and in the knowledge a Norwegian weather girl would accompany me. Mmm.

I collected Birgit from Heathrow on the Friday evening and we went out for a drink and a meal in that great Kent night spot that is Bexley. We arrived early for the game and I introduced her to the rest of the OLAS crew. Her ticket was in the upper tier of the Bobby Moore Stand, so we parted company for the game itself. West Ham raced into a 2-0 lead, Goddard – sorry, Kitson – scoring both. We were looking classy. Early in the second half,

Hugo won us yet another penalty with his trickery. With no Dicksy on the pitch, Hartson was the nominated penalty taker but with Kitson on a hat-trick, he handed the ball to a less than enthusiastic 'Kits'. He missed of course, but we didn't worry unduly, as Everton did not look much of a threat.

But when they scored with five minutes to go and started bombing forward, the writing was on the wall. The ball pinged about like a pinball in the penalty area in added time, Duncan Ferguson seizing on it and banging in the equaliser. West Ham had committed professional suicide. Later I thought about it. I still felt we had a better than even chance of staying up but if we did go down by one point, the little shake of the head Kitson gave Hartson as he offered him the ball would haunt me forever.

Birgit supported a Norwegian team from Oslo called Valerenga. That day I was proudly sporting the Valerenga tee-shirt she had bought me and when I met her in the Boleyn pub after the game I was mobbed by a bunch of nutty Norwegians who couldn't believe an English guy had a Valerenga tee-shirt. Such was their disbelief, they all had their photos taken with me.

I whisked Birgit reluctantly out of the pub to head off for a dinner appointment with George at Scribes. At least, we thought we did. We turned up to find a notice on the door informing us Venables had sold up and the club was shut for the foreseeable. Never mind, Café Rouge was a more than suitable replacement. We talked football long into the night and exchanged signed copies of our books. All very luvvy.

I left Birgit to her own devices for a few days. She was trying to sort out a college course and had some other friends to catch up with, while I had work to consider. We went and watched the film *Fever Pitch* in Leicester Square and I reluctantly have to say I thoroughly enjoyed it, although the casting of Colin Firth as Nick Hornby made me chuckle. It was stretching the imagination just a little.

Leicester City beckoned and it was my turn to drive. I picked up The Tortoise and headed over to Kev's, who kind of floated out of his front door. We had been an hour later than anticipated, in which time Kev had cracked open a bottle of red and had succeeded in getting completely off his face. This could have gone one of two ways, Either he could have been very aggressive and offensive, or, as it turned out, groovy and mellow, insisting that I put his Grateful Dead album on the tape player. I reluctantly agreed.

On arrival in Leicester we performed the biggest blag of the season to date. We were all in need of a piss, yet it was far too early to go inside the stadium. The only pub near the ground is The Turnstile, a known favourite haunt of the notorious Leicester City 'Baby Squad.' An appropriate name, as the whole concept is a little childish. We approached the stuffed shirt on the door and pleaded with him to let us in, do the necessary, then we would leave. He reluctantly agreed. After all, what trouble could three harmless looking, neutrally clothed, blokes and a Norwegian weather girl do in five minutes?

Once in, though, we decided we rather liked it. Picking a spot out of the line of vision of Mr Bouncer, we stayed for the duration. Chances were things would not continue in that vein, but they did. With time running out, West Ham won a throw-in. Harry urged the players to wait for Steve Lomas to jog forward and take the throw. The ball landed in the middle of the box at the feet of Moncur, who scored his second goal of the season and his second against Leicester. Justifiably, we went bananas.

Post-match interviews were revealing. Hugo gave an emotional monologue about how much he loved the fans at West Ham – yeah, yeah, Hugo, we heard that one from Slaven. In fairness to him, though, he was merely on loan and had a plethora of offers available to him in the summer. He was not going to commit himself. Bilic, on the other hand, appeared to have committed himself to Everton for the start of next season.

I hated him with a passion. I didn't blame him for the way things were going but I felt he had made a fool of me. I had worshipped him, sold my soul to him, bought a Croatian shirt to be like him, and now he had done this to me. I felt betrayed, helpless and a little bit cheap. In Sheffield, Nikki had done the same thing to me, but at least I'd got a shag out of it.

Birgit returned to hurdy-gurdy land and Kev and I spent a spare Saturday at Craven Cottage watching Fulham beat Hull City 2-0. That Duane Darby looked shit. Thank God we never signed him.

The ticket office phoned and confirmed my tickets for Old Trafford were ready for collection. I breathed a huge sigh of relief as Kev, Matt and Helen put away their knives.

28. Lovefool

West Ham United 5 Sheffield Wednesday 1 3.5.97

Stuart, the QPR fan, moved to Peterborough to live with his new woman, Jill. I had doubted her existence, as he had often mentioned her but she was never anywhere to be seen. To shut me up, he invited me up to celebrate his birthday and share a meal with the two of them and two of their friends, Mike and Nicola.

First on the agenda for the Saturday, though, was the home game with Sheffield Wednesday. A win would virtually guarantee safety, as long as Middlesbrough lost.

The Hammers put on a breathtaking display, Kitson finally bagging that hat-trick to become the first West Ham player to achieve the feat in the top flight since Tony Cottee in January 1986. Hartson bagged the other two to leave their combined total for the season standing at 13. The goals that ultimately saved West Ham from relegation.

We left Upton Park that Saturday afternoon with the blood racing through our veins and fixed grins apparent everywhere. Those smiles dropped a few minutes later, as we heard a late Ravanelli penalty had given 'Boro victory over Aston Villa at The Riverside, so our survival was still not a mathematical certainty. With tough matches against Newcastle United and Manchester United to come, we were going to need at least a point.

I put it to the back of my mind for a while to celebrate Stuart, the QPR fan's, birthday and finally meet the lovely Jill. We went out for a Chinese meal and I'm told I embarrassed myself in front of the waiter, although I have no recollection of that. Still, I know Stuart would never lie to me, so I suppose it must be true. Mike and Nicola were engaged to be married, and I gave Mike a copy of my book. I didn't realise he was going to read it all through his honeymoon. Sorry, Nicola.

Uncle Rupert covered our match with the Magpies and Brita came down from Wales to collect her prize of an audience with Julian Dicks. The match finished 0-0, which still wasn't a guarantee of safety, but it was going to take some pretty freakish results to send us down now. In fact, the following day our survival in the top flight was guaranteed as Middlesbrough played out a 0-0 draw at Blackburn Rovers – ironically, fulfilling the fixture they had failed to some months ago, costing themselves three crucial points in the process.

Kev fed me constant updates on the score as I sat in a meeting with Steve Blowers and a bloke called Alan Smith at BAFTA, of all places. Not the Arsenal striker with the big nose who scored the winner in the Cup Winners' Cup final, but a bicycle repair man from Norwich who had read my book and wanted to make a short film of it with the aid of a £10,000 grant from Anglia TV. Steve and I thought he was nuts but allowed him to submit his proposal. Neither of us was too shocked and I wasn't too disappointed when it was rejected.

Middlesbrough's inability to win at Ewood Park meant we were safe and could enjoy our trip to Old Trafford in comfort. And comfort it certainly was as we enjoyed a barbecue at Matt and Helen's house on the Saturday, before Matt drove us up to Mancland in his shiny new Mercedes, with posh leather seats, air conditioning, a fridge and an engine you could hardly hear.

It was another day of Manc title celebrations but we

tried not to let that bother us as we waved to the battalions of riot police that greeted us at the away end. What did they think we had in mind?

We lost 2-0 but, hey, who cares? We could laugh in comfort at Middlesbrough, relegated courtesy of a three-point deduction from the Premier League for non-fulfilment of their earlier fixture at Blackburn. We could laugh at Tottenham, beaten on the final day by Coventry City to ensure their own survival, and we could chuckle at Sunderland, who thought a draw at Wimbledon was enough, until they heard the news from White Hart Lane.

Football is funny. Sometimes.

29. I'll Be There For You

Espanyol Veterans 1 Charlton Athletic Veterans 1

A colleague of mine, Lindsay Hammill, played veterans' league football for Eynsford, a small Kent village. In a convoluted route, which took many twists, Eynsford Vets had been invited to join Charlton Athletic Vets on a tour of Barcelona, where they would take part in a four-team tournament at the Olympic hockey stadium.

As I had done some freelance journalism and had a book published, Lindsay had the idea that I could come along on the tour, do a write-up and get some publicity for the team and their fund-raising activities. I searched around and struck a deal with *FourFourTwo* magazine, who agreed to run an article on the trip. Charlton were to play an additional game, against Espanyol Vets, before the tournament started.

This being a football tournament, the first stop on arrival in Barcelona was, naturally, the bar. We had been there no more than five minutes, when who should walk past but Manchester United's Jordi Cruyff. I had my tape machine with me and the lads encouraged me to follow him into the bar and ask him for an interview. To my astonishment he agreed and I got a good 10 minutes out of him.

On the second day of the tour we were invited to meet Bobby Robson at the Nou Camp. We watched Barcelona training for a while, then Bobby came and spoke to us. I say, us, he really came to speak to Keith

Peacock. I just stood behind and pretended to be important. Robson, noticing we had no official guide, gave us a tour of the stadium and an insight into what it must be like to be a manager of such a huge club. He posed for a million photographs and signed everything in sight. He must have been pleased, for once, to meet some people who didn't want to beat the crap out of him. He had already won one trophy, was about to win another, but was going to lose out in the race for the *La Liga* title to Real Madrid. Not good enough.

I laughed inwardly and wondered what would have happened to him if Barca had endured a season like West Ham had just experienced.

At 5.30pm we departed for, we thought, Espanyol's ground, for Charlton's game against their vets. Instead the coach driver took us to a ghost town area of the city, differing from Peckham only in temperature. The Charlton players and their wives sat in slack-jawed disbelief as they were asked to perform on a pitch surrounded by stray dogs, tower blocks, supermarket trolleys and burning mattresses. The playing surface was, however, immaculate and the Eynsford boys drooled with jealousy, knowing their two games were to be played on astroturf.

The starting Charlton line-up was as follows: Bob Bolder, John Humphrey, Mike Bailey, Ritchie Bowman, Alan Curbishley, Mike Flanagan, Steve Gritt, Mark Penfold, Alan Pardew, Colin Walsh, Trevor Aylott. Subs: John Bumstead, Keith Peacock, Peter Hunt.

The game ended 1-1 and was great to watch, Aylott scoring Charlton's goal, despite being booked three times and never actually having played a first team game for the south London club. We kept quiet about that.

Back to the grim reality of Espanyol's training ground. We left the players and their emotionally drained spouses to tuck into a meal that wouldn't have looked out of place at Alcatraz.

The Charlton boys were distressed that we hadn't been invited to join them – not because of the affinity that had grown between us over the previous 24 hours, but because they knew they had to stay put, while we were off to hit Planet Hollywood.

The four-cornered contest at the Olympic hockey stadium kicked off with Charlton drawing 1-1 with Sabadell, before winning a penalty shootout. Jeff Wood was the hero. That being the case, Eynsford knew that victory against the home side, Terrassa, would ensure them a place in the final with Charlton. They would have done, too, had they not conceded six lucky goals.

The next day, after a magnificent pep talk from Keith Peacock, the Eynsford boys did themselves proud, losing by the odd goal in seven in the 3rd/4th-place play-off. Charlton won the tournament, beating Terrassa 2-1 in the final with goals from Steve Gritt and Alan Pardew.

It was a fantastic few days. We rubbed shoulders and dined with ex-professionals, who treated us as their equals, not an inconvenient bunch of hangers-on. They loved talking about their professional days and didn't mind that we kept asking them questions. Come the end of the tournament, the Charlton boys took us out to celebrate with a slap-up meal in a seafood restaurant. Aware that I had to write a serious(ish) article about the trip, I returned to Charlton's training ground at New Eltham a few days later to interview Curbishley and Peacock. On contacting *FourFourTwo* magazine to inform them of my return, they asked for copy with 24 hours. Working like a demon to produce the article overnight, they then decided not to run the piece. Not sure if *FourFourTwo* is the magazine's title, or their circulation figure these days.

Having spent some time with Curbishley and Peacock, I had been impressed with their views on the game. "I wouldn't be surprised if Charlton get promotion this year," I told Kev. He just laughed and told me not to be so silly.

30. Bitter Sweet Symphony

Barnsley 1 West Ham United 2   9.8.97

I prayed for some sort of consistency. The end to the season we had just experienced was all very well but it would have been nice to have gathered the points at a more even rate.

In a decision that baffled everyone, Hugo Porfirio decided against staying at Upton Park. Playing in the snow at Wrexham had obviously been too much for him and he decided on a move to Spanish club Racing Santander instead. His loss. Slaven Bilic also got his dream move to a big club. If you define 'big club' as being a club prepared to pay ridiculously inflated wages to over-rated bags of shite who inevitably let you down, then Everton are indeed a big club. One of the biggest in the world, in fact. Danny Williamson had also been linked to a move to Everton but this was not, I suspect, his dream.

Harry bought Eyal Berkovic, the little Israeli midfielder who had ripped us apart at The Dell last season, for a bargain £1.5m. Even better than the fact he had joined for such a small fee was the realisation that he had turned down Tottenham, possibly the logical choice for an Israeli, in order to join us. Craig Forrest, the Canadian international goalkeeper, arrived in a £500,000 move from Ipswich Town, while there was talk in the papers of moves for Newcastle United veterans Stuart Pearce and John Barnes. The Barnes deal was almost done and dusted when Kenny Dalglish waved a huge wad of cash and Barnes suddenly decided living in the north-east of England might be more interesting. It's curious that Harry consistently claims Dalglish is a good mate of his, yet he seems to spend most of his time stitching 'H' up.

The pre-season matches began early, with no major summer international tournament for players to be involved in, and we started our warm-up at Purfleet in mid-July with a comfortable 4-0 win. French defender David Terrier, on loan from Metz, made his first appearance, while David Absolem, another Israeli who was over on trial, also played. That proved to be the only friendly I managed to get to.

With the words of my new sales manager, Roger, ringing in my ears, namely that the season didn't start until August 9, so what did I want half-a-day off to go to Maidenhead for? Gary and the OLAS gang managed to get to 25 games of various descriptions in pre-season. I wasn't sure whether to be impressed or sympathetic. I did get to Pottsy's testimonial against QPR – a crowd of over 10,000 underlining the esteem in which he is held at Upton Park.

I had only ever once seen every single game in a season. That occurred in 1986-87. I had come close in the previous two years, missing two in 1995-96 and just one in 1996-97. I decided to go for it in 1997-98 and try to make every single match. To that end I bought an away season ticket, as well as a home one. This was a new idea and having spent many an unhappy hour queuing at Upton Park for tickets to games that were doomed to end in miserable defeat, I felt I had earned the right to have them land on my doorstep for a change.

Kev decided, or rather Kev's wife Jackie decided, that I had been single for far too long, so she proceeded to set me up in one of those obvious dinner party-type situations. The hosts just happen to invite two single people, discreetly withdraw to the kitchen and wait for nature to take its course. It wasn't quite like that.

A hot July evening in Turnpike Lane, in the back garden of Kev's new three bedroom house, the four of us sat sipping wine and making polite conversation. Angie was a colleague of Jackie's, the archetypal blonde nurse (what is it with me and nurses?), slim and attractive, that most men would die for and who, in truth, I found extraordinarily attractive. Her broad Ulster brogue was also a bit of a turn on but being a shy cove, I found it very difficult to make conversation and was relieved when Kev suggested we all go to the pub for a few looseners.

By the time we returned we were all a lot more relaxed, joined by Italian John and his missus, next door neighbours Javed and Sally and a Turkish bloke called Billy, who was a really great laugh. Turnpike Lane is a truly cosmopolitan area but everyone seems to get on okay. I was getting on fine with Angie at last, as I joined her on a trip to the newsagent to buy some fags and stopped to get even friendlier on the way home. I was drunk as a skunk, so was she, and by the time we returned to the garden, everyone else had gone home or gone to bed. By the time we eventually went to bed, the sun was coming up and the birds were singing. Kev shouted something at me at about 9am, when I extracted myself from Angie's bed with a thumping headache, to find Kev fully washed, dressed and breakfasted, suggesting we drive to Upton Park to sort out our away season tickets. I wanted to tell him to piss off but he was my host, so I stuck my head under the tap, put on some clothes and reluctantly got in the car.

By the time we returned I had recovered sufficiently to be sitting in the garden sipping a glass of red, when Angie came down and we hit that awkward silence. I gave her a lift home. Nothing of the previous night had been mentioned. When I reminded her, she claimed

100% memory loss. That was okay, I took the hint. When I got home I looked in the mirror to check I didn't have 'Mug' tattooed across my forehead.

The Barnsley tickets turned up with only a day or so to spare and despite the good finish to the previous season, I wasn't comfortable with the idea of an opening match at Oakwell. Newly-promoted and brimming with confidence after being used to winning for a whole year, I sensed impending disaster. Not only that, we hadn't won away on the opening day for nearly 25 years, so the omens were not good.

The consistency I yearned for was at least present in the form of the OLAS away trip. I picked Kev up to find he had borrowed the kids' temporary hair dye, and coloured his hair orange and green. As an OLAS veteran, I was largely excused selling duties before away matches and concentrated on getting pissed with Kev. We found a nice pub and got chatting to a very attractive lady. I say attractive, my memory is not so good these days, but I remember she was wearing denim shorts with frayed edges – that's enough to cloud anyone's judgement. She was convinced the game would finish 1-1, Barnsley would end up mid-table and just miss out on Europe. Doubled up in pain from suppressed laughter, we took our seats to witness Barnsley, as I had feared, starting like a train. Neil Redfearn opened the scoring with a header that looped over Ludo, giving the Tykes the half-time advantage.

In the second half, for once it was the opposition who hit the self destruct button. Their 'keeper came out for a cross on the edge of the box, only for John Boy Hartson to beat him to it and nod the ball into an empty net. Just 10 minutes from time, Frank Lampard, making his first senior appearance since breaking his leg at Villa Park, scored with his second touch to send the travelling fans wild and infuriate the locals, who felt he may have handled the ball.

Outside, it was hard not to gloat, so we didn't try. I grabbed a quick interview with Pottsy and tried to speak to Berkovic, who pretended he couldn't speak English. We also grabbed a word with Alan Wilkie, the referee, who revealed that this had been the first game he'd refereed involving Hartson where he hadn't booked him. Joint top of the table, the ride home was all the sweeter for the knowledge that our next match was to be against a Spurs team so disorganised, they made the Keystone Cops look like the Italian national side.

It didn't take long. Just two minutes, in fact, for Hartson to double his tally for the season and put us one up against Spurs. Steffen Iversen was lucky to escape more than a booking after making a gesture, which clearly questioned the linesman's personal habits. No action was taken, even though video evidence was categorical. I felt a little aggrieved, feeling sure that had it been Julian Dicks, he'd be facing an eight-match ban. No matter, Berkovic scored a sweet second to re-enforce his allegiance to the Hammers and stick two fingers up at the club he rejected. Les Ferdinand pulled one back but it was too little, too late for Spurs. Their opening day defeat to the Mancs meant they were pointless after two games. I laughed and laughed and laughed.

Danny Williamson had made the move to Everton but, we sensed, in something of an arm-lock. David Unsworth and a million quid came in the other direction. We thought we had the better end of the deal at first but after seeing what turned out to be a rhinoceros in white shorts playing on a regular basis, I wasn't so sure. The bizarre prospect of two players each making their debuts against their former colleagues beckoned as West Ham travelled to Goodison Park. Everton had keeled over spectacularly in their opening game against

Crystal Palace and we hoped for more of the same as a free-kick from Hartson headed for the corner flag, only to be diverted into his own goal by Dave Watson. That mouthy lot in the Gwladys Street end were beautifully quiet. They stuck up for Slaven, though, as you might expect, but the abuse we hurled at him was more in jest than anything else. There is a part of you that hopes beyond hope that players will do the decent thing and stay on. But when you are dealing with a footballer, and a bloke, what chance have you got of finding any loyalty?

Everton won the match 2-1, reminding us that we probably weren't so clever after all. Unsworth had made a steady debut but seemed a lot faster after the game than he was during it, as Craig and I chased him around the block for an interview. Gary caught a few words with Williamson, who didn't say so in as many words but looked genuinely depressed and burdened by the price tag put on his head. We even managed a few stuttering words from Mr Bilic. Like an ex-lover explaining her reasons for running off with another man, he told us: "I felt suffocated in our relationship, I needed to breathe." None of his words impressed us.

By the time we got back to London we were heartily sick of *Be Here Now*, the new Oasis album. By Wednesday this had been replaced for the trip to Coventry by *Eighties Soul Weekender*, hurdly an adequate substitute in my view. I was happy to retreat to the pub with Kev and new OLAS writer Jon Jacques.

This away season ticket lark proved to be quite useful, as Kev and I took our seats to find ourselves in the front row of the upper tier, as we had done at Goodison. The perfect nature of the view meant we could see just how lethargic we were in the first half, conceding a goal by Darren Huckerby just before half time. Second half, and Stan Lazaridis turned on a great display to run the show for West Ham. Despite the introduction of super-sub Dowie, we still equalised, through a header from Kitson.

The last Saturday of August saw us roll Wimbledon over in the gutter, 3-1. Dons' boss Joe Kinnear complained the first goal had been offside but he could have no grounds for complaint over the whole 90 minutes. West Ham played with a patience, a maturity and style that had been lacking in the opening stages of previous seasons, but a worrying inability to keep a clean sheet was a traditional trait, and one that would continue to date. Rieper provided us with a parting gift before leaving for Celtic, Hartson and Berkovic netting the others.

The next morning I was woken early by a phone call from my father, who told me that Diana, Princess of Wales, had been killed in a car crash in Paris. It was indeed a shock, and very sad, but I felt the country over-reacted in a pretty huge way. Although the nation loved her, you couldn't help but feel she was a scheming little minx at times, using the fact she had the press wrapped around her little finger to her advantage. It is doubtful though, had she lived, influential as she was, whether even she could have found us a shirt sponsor.

In a farce that could only happen at West Ham, Dagenham Motors' offer of another year of shirt sponsorship was rejected, as it seemed we had bigger fish to fry. The rumour was that a South African airline would be the new sponsor, in deal that was "99% certain to be in place for the Tottenham game." Well, to be fair, the club didn't say which Tottenham game, or which season. The South African airline's logo never appeared on a West Ham shirt, so we went through a whole season without a main sponsor.

Barcelona didn't have a shirt sponsor either. But there the similarity with West Ham ended.

31. Men In Black

Arsenal 4 West Ham United 0 24.9.97

Rio Ferdinand's selection for the England squad was obviously too much to take for the poor lad, and within seconds he was done for drink-driving. Banned for a year, and handed a £500 fine, now England coach Glenn Hoddle taught Rio the lesson of his life and removed his name from the squad as an example to others. Still, wife-beater Gazza, reformed alcoholic and motor-wrecker Tony Adams and coke-snorting Merson were nevertheless in the squad, so no double standards there, which was good to see. Maybe Rio had also been bad in a previous life.

It was the start of Black September. Rio's exclusion from the England squad was nothing compared to the disastrous string of games that was to follow. We trekked back up to Old Trafford to watch Hartson catch out the United defence and the dozy cameraman to put us ahead. Kitson fluffed a gilt-edged chance to make it two and United took over. The snarling, arrogant, mouthy Roy Keane hit a speculative shot and Moncs diverted it past a stranded Ludo for their equaliser. Scholes scored the winner with a header and Kits missed another good chance to give us a point. But this was Old Trafford, 'Theatre of Dreams'. Theatre of Dreams indeed. Arrogant gobshites.

The following Tuesday saw us hitting the motorways again, for a first-ever visit to the new McAlpine Stadium in Huddersfield for the first leg of our Coca-Cola Cup-tie.

Kitson withdrew with a late injury and we looked crap again. Where was that consistency I longed for? Huddersfield Town didn't look all that great either but a goal from Alex Dyer near the end gave them a 1-0 first leg victory and made us realise there was still a hell of a lot of work to be done. There was still a hell of a long drive too. Huddersfield is a bloody long way.

Newcastle United were next up at The Boleyn. I met Dr Sik for a drink before the game, explaining to him in great detail why Newcastle would lose, because West Ham were just so invincible at home, not losing a home match since the end of January. Ian Pearce, another big money signing (what, another sofa?) from Blackburn Rovers, made his debut. He played in defence and, to be fair to the lad, he looked highly suspect. West Ham tore Newcastle apart for 89 minutes but in that one minute when the Magpies got forward, they scored, Asprilla shielding the ball in a suspiciously Colombian way, allowing John Barnes to ping one into the top corner.

It was depressing to think that after spending all that money we were still a bit crap. Players who had dumped on us to sign elsewhere were still coming back to haunt us, and players we were signing for silly money were turning out to be donkeys. Still, we had Arsenal to come on the Wednesday night. A guaranteed three points for us, if you work by the adage that says when you think West Ham are going to get stuffed, they usually win. This was the exception that proved the rule.

We thought we would get trounced and we were – 4-0 down at half time, Pearce looked hopelessly out of his depth as Dutch duo Overmars and Bergkamp ripped us to shreds. To compound our misery, Big Mouth Wright scored from the spot and we watched the second half through our fingers, like a five-year-old might watch Dr Who. The fact Arsenal did not add to their score was more down to the fact they were taking it easy rather than any fantastic display of defending by us. In fact, Hartson looked as though he wished he could still be playing for Arsenal and inexplicably whacked the ball into touch for a corner – from the halfway line! He later claimed to have been aiming for Steve Bould's head. If he had been, he missed by a mile. Things really were looking bad.

The night was summed up by some rare humour from the Arsenal fans on the clock end who, to the tune of *Let's All Do The Conga*, chanted *We've Got Dennis Bergkamp*, quickly followed by *You've got Iain Dowie!*

The arrival of Andrew Impey was not likely to improve things. Impey arrived from QPR a few weeks previously and in the traditional manner of most big money Hammers signings, promptly declared himself injured. 'Hammertoes' was the slightly baffling explanation given in the papers for Impey's prolonged absence. I wondered if the story hadn't been written by a slightly deaf journalist, and if Impey was suffering from nothing more than halitocis.

Whatever he'd been suffering from, he made his debut against Liverpool and actually looked like he might be a bit useful, shaving the bar with a rising drive in the first half. Hartson put us ahead with a tap in, the ball rebounding perfectly off the post into his path. Maybe our luck was changing. Or maybe not, as Robbie Fowler fired an exocet of a volley in to equalise. To their credit, despite being atrocious in the last few away games, we had been outstanding at home all season, even in the Newcastle match we had lost. It was no surprise when Berkovic grabbed his second for the club to restore out lead, win the game and at last give us some points in September. The boost was much needed. After reaching third place by beating Wimbledon, defeat by Arsenal had seen us slump to

10th. I reasoned that only a few months previously, I would have killed for 10th place. But then a few months previously, we hadn't spent £15m on players.

The month closed with a comfortable 3-0 win in the second leg of the cup-tie with Huddersfield. Uncle Rupert, sensing an upset, had his cameras there, but they only witnessed a Hartson hat-trick, to take us comfortably through to the next round and a home tie against Aston Villa. Sorry to disappoint you, Rupert.

32. Tubthumping

Leicester City 2 West Ham United 1 27.10.97

It was a bit like the old days, winning at home and getting spanked away. It was as though two completely different teams took to the field. The Jekyll and Hyde nature of West Ham's performances was never better illustrated than in October, which began with complete humiliation at The Dell. It's easy to understand why we might have a mental block when it comes to playing at venues like Old Trafford, Anfield or St James' Park. But quite why we should always play quite so badly at The Dell remains a mystery. In a tiny stadium more suited to the Nationwide Conference than the Premiership, we have consistently failed to win since a Chapman and Morley double gave us a 2-0 victory there in November 1993. Not only that, we have consistently played like hopeless imbeciles on each visit, this one being no exception, and Southampton clobbered us 3-0.

With a blank Saturday due to internationals – England confirming their place at the World Cup finals with a highly creditable 0-0 draw in Italy – the more acceptable face of West Ham showed itself as Villa were beaten out of sight in the Coca-Cola Cup at Upton Park. Two from John Boy and one from the fast improving Lampard sealed a place in the fourth round against Walsall, again at Upton Park, offering the very real possibility of a quarter-final appearance.

The first clean sheet of the campaign coincided with the debut of Canadian Craig Forrest in goal. He repeated the feat a few days later against Bolton Wanderers and it seemed the writing was on the wall for Ludo.

Bolton were also spanked 3-0. Hartson's brace taking his season's total to date to 12, more than any of our top scorers had managed in the previous three seasons, and this was only October. Berkovic scored the other in a bad tempered game that saw Gerry Taggart sent off.

Uncle Rupert intervened once again for the game with Leicester City at Filbert Street. He decided it would be really boring to allow West Ham fans the luxury of a leisurely trip up the M1 on a Saturday or Sunday morning, thinking it would be much more fun to make them take an afternoon off work and drive up in the rush hour. Bastard. Still Kev and me at last found a pub in Leicester that was within walking distance of the ground, and was also reasonably friendly. We toyed with the idea of trying The Turnstile again but the absence of a Norwegian weather girl put us off. At last we put in an away performance that could justifiably be called a 'performance.' We went 1-0 down to a goal from Emile Heskey, which still looks offside to this day whenever I see it, but no-one ever says anything because it's Heskey, and he's in the England fold now, and pretty soon he'll be allowed to get away with murder.

We played well in the second half and deservedly drew level when Berkovic scored, running to the crowd to collect an Israeli flag to drape over his shoulders. I worried that this might be an indication he was home sick, or that he wanted to go to Tottenham after all. West Ham just couldn't hang on, though, and former Oldham Athletic nemesis Ian Marshall scored after some penalty box pinball, despite having 14 defenders on the line. We were just not meant to get anything away from home. To add insult to injury, Hartson branded referee Mike Reid a 'homer', insinuating he favoured the home side – not that he was a fat, yellow, slobby American TV cartoon character.

Another signing ended October. Samassi Abou arrived for what appeared to be a bargain £250,000 after the initial asking price had been £400,000. Small change for the Cockney boys by the standards of 1997.

Uncle Rupert was on our case, big time. Our home match against Crystal Palace also received the Monday Night Special treatment. Quite what was special about the visit of Palace remained a mystery. Their form mirrored West Ham's. They were winning away but hadn't won a game at home. Something had to give. It looked like our home form was going to collapse as Shipperley put Palace into a 2-0 lead. Abou made his debut in the second half, while the arrival of Impey provided some impetus, as Hartson nodded in an Unsworth freekick to reduce the arrears and Abou set Lampard up on the edge of the box to slam home the equaliser. No sooner had Lampard run to the West Lower to milk the applause, Boom! Out went the lights.

Floodlights are funny things. Apparently you can't just switch them on and off willy-nilly, like you can your bedside lamp. Oh no. Floodlights are shy, sensitive creatures and they get hotter than your average 60w pearl lightbulb from Woolies. That being the case, after a delay of about 15 minutes, we were informed the game was to be abandoned, so all the statistics were wiped from the record books. It later transpired that a Far Eastern betting syndicate had pulled the plug in order to collect on the draw.

I took The Wonderful Helen to witness a spectacular firework display on Blackheath. Before hand we had walked around the village, arms linked, cuddled up together sheltering from the rain under a big golfing umbrella. It was very romantic. As we sat in the car to watch the fireworks, I yearned for the chance to show her some of my own, but it wasn't going to happen. My chances with The Wonderful Helen were about as good as West Ham's away form.

The following Sunday was an away game and, therefore, a defeat. Chelsea were the lucky owners of the winning ticket this time, although with the game 0-0 at half time, it looked like we might be able to scrape something. Ruud Gullit was aware of the problem and within 35 minutes had made a substitution. Chelsea re-grouped and by the time we had cottoned on, we were two down. Rio was unlucky to deflect a Zola cross past Forrest into his own goal but Zola's free-kick was sheer class. Spotting Hartson moving off the goal line, he bent the ball precisely into the space John Boy had occupied a few seconds before. We fell apart and had to endure the embarrassing sight of Moncur and Berkovic squaring up to each other. Not a good sign. Abou won us our first penalty of the season, which Hartson dispatched less than convincingly to put a gloss of respectability to the scoreline, but in truth we had been comprehensively beaten.

Rio finally sobered up in time to be picked for the England squad to face Cameroon in a friendly at Wembley. With Southgate limping off injured, he made his debut and gave an assured performance in the 2-0 win. It is a pity that every England manager since Ramsey has consistently failed to recognise the talents of West Ham players when preparing for major tournaments. Everyone knows England don't win trophies unless they have three West Ham players in the team. We may have said that in jest in the past but now, when we had a player who was potentially the cultured defender England had been screaming out for, every excuse in the book was dredged up to stop him playing. Old has-beens such Adams, Keown and Southgate continued to get the nod. The establishment rules. Percentage management at its worst. Just because we are winning, it doesn't mean we can't improve. It makes me sick.

Walsall arrived at Upton Park with memories of our previous encounter in the competition no doubt still fresh in their minds and harbouring hopes of a repeat performance. For once the plucky underdog came a cropper against West Ham and they were beaten 4-1, a hat-trick from Frank Lampard and the inevitable Upton Park goal from Hartson.

I haven't mentioned work for a while. That's probably because up to this point things were going well. On my new agency I was bringing in plenty of new business, so much so that I was awarded the dubious honour of a day out at Blackburn Rovers, in the hospitality suite, to witness their game against Chelsea. With West Ham not due to play until the Sunday – another live TV game against Leeds United at Elland Road – I took the chance to claim some outrageous expenses and drove up to Blackburn on the Saturday morning. After a tour of the stadium, we sat down to a superb meal, chatting with former Rovers player Stuart Metcalfe. Currently working as a nurse in a mental home and working at Rovers on matchdays to earn a few extra bob, it brought home to me as we sat in the lap of luxury, enjoying the trappings of wealth, how the game had changed – and not necessarily for the better.

The curtains pulled back, we watched the game through glass in a sterile atmosphere. After all, who wants to mix with those common, poor people in the stands? I felt as though I was betraying my own kind a little, but satisfied myself that Chelsea were losing 1-0 to a brilliant strike from Gary Croft and I was sitting next to two Chelsea fans. My time was not wasted, as I constantly took the piss out of them.

We voted Tim Flowers man-of-the-match and he came up to our box to receive his prize and jump through the hoops that players have to these days. It wouldn't surprise me if a lot of players deliberately play shit to avoid winning these prizes and having to make small talk with a bunch of people who probably know next to nothing about the game.

But it's these people who pay the wages, so the players have to pay lip service to them, at least. It's an unholy mess.

I scooted back down the A1 and spent the night at Stuart, the QPR fan's, new home in Lincolnshire, to save going all the way back home again before travelling back up to Leeds again on the Sunday.

The stewards at Leeds were being absolute petty minded arseholes, kicking people out for minor offences. We were not in the best of moods, until Lampard raced onto a second half through ball and tucked it away. He steamed over to the corner flag and danced around it, just as his dad, Frank Senior, had done 17 years before. It was a pity but his team-mates obviously didn't realise the significance of his actions as they mobbed him before he had a chance to complete the move.

A shame also that his colleagues then decided to play like a bunch of headless chickens, conceding the game in a 3-1 defeat. Kev and I were heading for the car as Hasselbaink grabbed his second and Leeds United's third. We had seen it before so many times, we didn't really want to have to sit through it again. Driving home, I was in no mood to compromise. As I raced through the roadworks on the M1, speed cameras flashed like a bank of paparazzi spotting Liz Hurley in a see-through dress. I got away with it. God only knows how.

At home to Villa the following Saturday, we approached December in 15th place. Not exactly earth shattering but all you can expect if you lose six away games on the spin.

Villa rolled over, 2-1, Hartson bagging another brace, his second arriving literally seconds after Dwight Yorke had equalised for Villa. Villa played much better than they had in the Coca-Cola Cup a few weeks before. But then, they couldn't have played much worse.

That night, The Wonderful Helen accompanied me to my work's Christmas bash – yes, on November 29. I was the proudest man in the room. Later that night, though, I laid my cards on the table. She showed me her hand, too, and seeing there could be no winner, we both decided to stack.

33. Perfect Day

West Ham United 4 Crystal Palace 1 3.11.97

December has always been a month in which West Ham have struggled. Usually lucky to get three points between December and March, we hit that target within three days, rearranging our aborted game with Crystal Palace. This time there were no scares. Unsworth and Berkovic carved Palace open, allowing Hartson to score an opener before Lazaridis proved that his right foot is for standing on, making a complete hash of a goal-line clearance and allowing Shipperley in to grab an equaliser. Stan made up for it, though, creating the opportunity for Berkovic to restore the lead, and West Ham never looked back. Unsworth and Lomas each added their first goals for the club, wrapping up an impressive 4-1 win.

After such a comprehensive victory, leaving aside all that had gone before on our travels that season, we could have been forgiven for thinking we had a chance of turning Derby County over at Pride Park. Ludo played in goal in what turned out to be his last game for the club. In a distinguished career with West Ham he made 365 appearances in all. A gentle giant, he was one of my favourite players of all time. I even named my cat after him. Never fussed, just got on with it, that was our Ludo. It was such a pity that his swansong should be marked with two such humongous errors. First he allowed Paulo Wanchope to beat him to a cross for the opening goal, then he bowled the ball straight out to Dean Sturridge, who took a few touches and buried it, along with West Ham's chances.

The highlight of the day was seeing Paulo Alves, the Portuguese international signed on loan. Not because his silky skills lit up the pitch on an otherwise dank, dark Saturday afternoon, but because the Derby fans mistook him for Paul Kitson – a hate figure among Derby fans who didn't appreciate his move to Newcastle United some years earlier. Kits and Alves both had black hair and a big nose but there the similarity ended. Alves was about a foot taller than Kitson and – here's the big clue to his identity – had a number 30 on his back and the word "ALVES" emblazoned across his shoulders. Even the thickest East Midlander should have been able to spot it but the Pride Park faithful didn't care. They were convinced this was their man and sang rude songs about him. That, and the fact Spurs lost 6-1 at home to Chelsea, made the trip home almost bearable.

A 1-0 win over Sheffield Wednesday followed. Can you guess the venue? That's right, Upton Park, and a sight for sore eyes as Kitson returned from injury to grab the winner in a scrappy game that could have gone either way. Having been smashed out of sight 5-1 at the end of last season, Wednesday were careful not to allow the same thing to happen again but they couldn't prevent Kitson nabbing the winner.

An unofficial OLAS Christmas party followed. Those present being primarily those that used to write for OLAS but had now shut up to allow the new breed to have their say. Me, Kev, Matt and Helen were joined by seller Wes, who wasn't invited but found us anyway and was more than welcome, a couple of people from Radio Five, and Chris (now curiously re-named Khris?) Raistrick from Clubcall. A bizarre evening ended in the Chinese restaurant, writing an article for OLAS on a paper napkin, which never did see the light of day.

153

Still one more game to deal with before tucking in to the Christmas turkey. The same guy at Lancaster Gate who sent us to Middlesbrough the day before Christmas Eve a couple of years back, must have been wetting himself laughing when he came up with Blackburn Rovers away for us on December 20. Not only was it a bloody long way, on a roll of seven straight away defeats it was also a guaranteed waste of time. For the first time that season, I considered going shopping instead, or putting my feet up and watching us get spanked on Teletext. However, I had decided to do every game, I had a ticket, so it would have been a shame to miss it. And after all, this is West Ham, so you never know.

I should have known. This time we were so poor even Stuart Ripley managed to score against us – his first goal for 253 years. Lomas got sent off for doing something we'd all like to have a go at, manhandling referee Gerald Ashby. Steve was understandably upset when a blatant penalty was not given but, as Paolo Di Canio found out to his cost, you toucha da referee, youze paysa da price.

On the way home we devised a system to save us fans having to make 500-mile round trips to watch games we knew damn well would end in defeat. Before the season starts, all the Premiership managers sit down and have a meeting. Those fixtures the managers know they will never win are by mutual consent conceded. It would work like this: Roy Hodgson would say to Harry: "Come on Hawwy, you know u never win here, let's have the thwee points and save ourselves a lot of time and effort..." Now if Harry agrees, Blackburn get thwee, sorry, three points and no more is said. If Harry doesn't agree and plays the game and loses, Blackburn get six points. If West Ham win, West Ham get six points. It could work, trust me. The only problem would be that Manchester United would probably only play half a dozen games a season.

With Ludo on the way out, Harry signed Bernard Lama, the French international goalkeeper, on loan from Paris St Germain.

Boxing Day provided me with the opportunity to take my dad to a game, and for Kev to celebrate his 40th birthday wearing a preposterous hat. An 11.30am kick-off meant that beers were hard to come by but that's never stopped Kev before. Kitson scored the winner for the second home game in a row and George Boateng tried to cripple Frank Lampard, taking the rest of the day off for his trouble. The points haul for December reached 12 when the drought of results away from home finally abated. Ben Thatcher, the former Millwall thug, was sent off in the opening minutes for elbowing Kitson. A farcical own goal and another from the boot of Kitson provided a 2-1 win and a first double of the season. It was a nice way to end the calendar year and proved to be another one of those turning points. We would lose only one more away game in the next three months. 1997 ended with West Ham in eighth place, playing good football and looking down at the relegation fight for a change. Happy New Year!

34. Never Ever

West Ham United 2 Emley 1   3.1.98

Brita came down for the cup-tie with non-league
Emley and, as usual, brought torrential rain with her. The
moment we heard the draw we all shuddered. After all,
with West Ham's record against lower division sides, this
was an accident waiting to happen. But this was a
different West Ham side. This was a West Ham side
eighth in the Premiership, unbeatable at home. Surely
we could not do anything other than win handsomely?

And it looked like we would win handsomely as
torrential rain poured out of a clear blue January
afternoon sky and made pretty rainbows above the East
Stand. When Lampard put us 1-0 up in the first few
minutes, it was surely going to be a question of how
many. Not so. A combination of factors, over-confidence
possibly being one of them, together with a waterlogged
pitch and the fact Emley were a lot better than we gave
them credit for, produced a nail biting match in which
the non-leaguers equalised and came very close to
taking us to a replay, scheduled for the McAlpine
Stadium, the scene of one embarrassing capitulation
already this season.

Our blushes were spared by Hartson, who scored the
winner late on. The record books show that West Ham
went through to the fourth round. They mention nothing
about the nature of the win. Probably just as well.

A busy schedule saw Arsenal next at Upton Park in
the quarter-finals of the Coke Cup. Despite a wretched

performance against Emley, we were confident we would play better against the Arse, with a semi-final place against Chelsea at stake. It started well enough, Seaman fouling Kitson to provide West Ham with the best opportunity they were likely to get in a tight first half. Hartson strode manfully up but scuffed the penalty so pathetically at Seaman, he practically had to come off his line to collect it. That was it. You don't get second chances against teams destined to win the double and before you could say "Rio made a cock-up", we were 2-0 down and staring elimination in the face. Abou came on and slipped between Keown and Adams to lob a goal back but Arsenal were totally in control. The last time we played Arsenal at Upton Park we had lost 2-1. We had improved by a country mile but the gap in class was still awesome. Back to the drawing board.

Abou was proving to be a hit with the fans with his deft flicks, scampering running style and a haircut Medusa would have been proud of, and the fact that when you chant his name it sounds like "A boooooooooooo". Little things please little minds. He hit the peak of his popularity the following Saturday. Still licking our wounds from defeat by Arsenal, Barnsley came to Upton Park experiencing a wretched run. It continued. West Ham took out all their frustrations on helpless Barnsley, thumping them 6-0. Lampard opened the scoring and Abou got the second and third with delightful strikes, set up with flowing football that left Barnsley in a spin. Moncur added his goal for the season, Hartson bagged the fifth and Lazaridis got in on the act at the very end to make it six. I didn't bother looking to find out the last time we'd scored six in a top-flight game. I wasn't sure if my records went back that far.

On the crest of a wave after scoring six, and with Tottenham wobbling so precariously they had turned in desperation to former hero Jürgen Klinsmann, it seemed they would be there for the taking at White Hart Lane. Not only that, but with the away hoodoo well and truly nailed, and a good recent record at The Lane, surely all three points were up for grabs. Well, they were, but for Tottenham. Klinsmann inevitably scuffed the winner, Abou was sent packing for a retaliatory kick at Vega, and Calderwood appeared to clear the ball from the Tottenham box using his fist. Altogether a pretty average away trip, really.

Abou refused to leave the pitch, much to the dismay of referee David Elleray. A minor skirmish ensued, with Harry getting himself involved on the touchline. Vega, who had appeared crippled following Abou's kick, miraculously recovered once the red card had been brandished and the Tottenham fans showed uncharacteristic generosity by showering us with their loose change.

We trudged back to Seven Sisters tube station, gloomily pondering the future and wondering if the win at Wimbledon had been a fluke. We were painfully aware that a tricky cup-tie at Maine Road was to follow the next Sunday.

By now, the OLAS away trip possé was bordering on the preposterously massive. We had no fewer than 12 regulars who wanted to make the trip to Maine Road, so, we felt the best way to handle it was to hire a minibus. Gary felt the best way to handle it was to let me hire a minibus, to be more accurate.

So, precariously driving a vehicle bigger than anything I had ever driven before, 11 friends and colleagues trusted me with their lives, as the bus chugged up the motorway on a sun-drenched Sunday morning. I had got used to the controls by the time we had reached Stoke and the stereo pumped out *OK Computer* by Radiohead, which, naturally, only pleased half of those present. Still, they were getting a comfortable trip to an away game for around £6 a head, so no one complained too much as the driver exercised his stereo-hogging privilege.

No such luck sneaking into the Kippax stand this time, even though we were early. Instead I dropped Gary and most of the gear at the away end, picked up our friends from the north, Liam and Sean, and found a car park that was prepared to take a bus.

We also found a convenient watering hole in the shape of the local sports centre, appropriately named The Oasis. City were struggling, despite having some classy players like Kinkladze, Uwe Rosler and, er, Jamie Pollock. City also have some classy fans, not like the sycophantic scumbags that haunt the stands of Old Trafford and the armchairs of the home counties. We engaged in some light banter with a few who hailed from Stockport. "Why don't you support Stockport then?" I asked, parodying the fact they always criticise United fans for coming from anywhere other than Manchester. Having established where I came from, he replied: "Why don't you support Charlton?" He had a fair point and, as a City fan, I guessed that, like my addiction to West Ham, he had not chosen to be in this predicament.

The match was a full-blooded FA Cup tie, the sort rarely seen these days. West Ham controlled early on, having a goal disallowed for offside, before Berkovic notched just as I had gone downstairs to get a pie. This was annoying. At the Barnsley game I had missed Abou's first through answering a call of nature, now this. Subsequent attempts to procure a goal by leaving my seat ended in failure but at that point it seemed I was doomed. My blushes were saved by the bloke in front of me in the queue for the pies, who had a hand-held TV and was able to show me the goal on the action replay. Isn't technology wonderful? Or rather, isn't it wonderful that football fans are now so stinking rich, they bring portable tellies to the game with them? No, it isn't wonderful really, is it?

At about this time, debate was raging over the so-called *Nouveau* supporter, the new breed pouring in from the home counties, claiming to have been West Ham fans all their lives and buying everything they could that was painted claret and blue. Yet, standing on their seat in the East Stand upper tier, they would shout: "Come on number 10!". It's not just Manchester United who have to endure their share of band-wagon-jumpers. I am sure there are many United fans who remember standing on the Stretford End to watch Second Division football in 1975, just as there are many United fans now who wouldn't believe you if you told them they had once been relegated.

Fans who don't know their club's history are one thing. Those who know nothing about the present are another, and should be exterminated – however much money they have.

I digress. City turned on the style in the second half and equalised with a fabulous strike from Kinkladze that won goal-of-the-season three years running. City then won a penalty. I groaned. Another away defeat beckoned. But Forrest stood tall in goal, stretched his arms above his head and they appeared to reach a good two feet above the crossbar. Rosler must have seen this and panicked, blasting his kick way above the bar. A replay seemed on but ex-City skipper Lomas had other ideas, drilling in a low strike to win the match. I was delighted and a little surprised. Not just that Lomas had managed to hit a shot that stayed low, but that we had turned around a potential defeat into glorious victory.

Outside we joined the City fans in their "Lee Out!" demonstrations and made more friendships in a relationship which had its genesis in the final game of the 1986-87 season.

New OLAS writer Ollie Steele interviewed Bernard Lama and Abou In fluent French, which revived memories of my pathetic attempts at interviewing Florin Raducioiu. Admittedly, French is a little different to Romanian but I was beginning to feel a little surplus to requirements, other than being a useful driver.

That being my job, I collected the minibus, a generous helping of mushy peas, chips and gravy and we trundled back to London secure in the knowledge that our fifth round tie would be at home to Sheffield Wednesday or Blackburn Rovers.

Trevor Sinclair joined West Ham during the week, in a player swap that saw Keith Rowland, Iain Dowie and £1.6m head the other way. Stuart, the QPR fan, was gutted, not just at losing Sinclair, but at gaining Dowie. I wasn't convinced we had the best deal in the world either. I had seen Sinclair a couple of times at QPR and he had looked, well, let's be fair, crap.

As he took to the field against Everton, though, he looked a different player. Beefy and strong, he'd lost the dreadlocks and at least appeared to be more serious about his game. The 90 minutes that followed proved he had, and that maybe a move was exactly what he needed to bring the best out of him. He scored twice on his debut, to secure a 2-2 draw against an Everton side who refused to lie down despite twice being behind. In truth, 2-2 was probably the best result we could have expected, for apart from Sinclair, the rest of the team didn't look up for it.

Still, there's always a silver lining. Tony Cottee had returned to England and joined Leicester City. He scored their winner at Old Trafford. Nice one, TC.

35. Gettin' Jiggy Wit It

Newcastle United 0 West Ham United 1 7.2.98

Despite buying Shearer and Gary Speed, and anyone or anything else that wasn't nailed down, Kenny Dalglish's Newcastle United side still looked a bit suspect. Not suspect enough to lose to West Ham, though, we asserted, as we drove up the A1 in Gary's Land Cruiser. Being cursed with short legs, I was relegated to the back seats, joined by Dan and a very poorly looking Wes who was complaining he was full of flu. Terrific, I thought, leg cramp, a stuffing by a second-rate Geordie side and a dose of flu to boot. Kev and I amused ourselves by taking the piss out of young Wes. Surely it couldn't be that bad? As we piled out of the bus in the Metro station car park, though, Wes collapsed in a pathetic heap on the floor. We hoped this was due to him feeling the effects of the flu, and not because we had been encouraging him to take liberal helpings of cold remedy, washed down with a bumper size can of Strongbow.

We left Wes to sleep it off and went to a restaurant Buzz had sampled on his last visit. Called Lucky Lukes, a buffet lunch was laid on with all-you-can-eat-for-a-fiver. Being in the shadow of the main stand, we didn't have to leave until 10 minutes before kick-off, by which time we had all eaten, and drunk, more than we possibly should have. Still, you can't watch West Ham on an empty stomach, it's bad for you.

Lazaridis hit a wonder strike from what appeared to

be the halfway line but was, in fact, about 30 yards and we danced in the aisles. Not for too long, though, too many servings of pizza won't allow it. Also, we knew our joy would probably be short-lived but to our amazement, despite the referee playing 15 minutes of injury time, Newcastle United were pathetically inept. Even Gary Speed, who nearly always scored against us when playing for Leeds United or Everton, failed spectacularly. Rio had England has-been Shearer in his pocket all afternoon and the three points put us in eighth place, just one point off sixth, and a possible UEFA Cup spot.

Outside the atmosphere was a little tense. Gary enjoyed a toe-to-toe conversation with a Geordie, who took exception to Gary's comment that Shearer was a 'wanker.' After debating the point nose to nose for some 10 minutes, we all shuffled into line behind Gary and the mouthy Geordie backed down, no doubt off to The Strawberry to tell his mates how he'd taken on seven Cockneys and won.

Stan was his usual modest self when interviewed afterwards but was desperate for a lift home so he could avoid flying. We didn't have any room but as I tucked my knees up under my chin next to a snuffling Wes for the second time that day, I wondered why I hadn't offered to swap with Stan. I always think of great ideas when it's too late.

Blackburn Rovers' triumph in the FA Cup at Hillsborough meant it was they who faced us on Valentine's Day at Upton Park in the fifth round. Kevin Gallacher gave them an early lead and we appeared to be in disarray. Running through the centre circle, Gallacher palmed off Berkovic and he went down like the proverbial sack of spuds. A red card ensued, which enraged all connected with Blackburn, giving West Ham the impetus to forge ahead. Kitson equalised, threading a delicate shot through a crowd of players, and before half-time Hartson's shot was deflected into the net by Berkovic to put us 2-1 up and seemingly into the hat for the last eight. Blackburn had other ideas, though, and Sutton's second half header was judged to have crossed the line before Forrest scooped it out. We left disappointed at the prospect of a replay, with our recent record at Ewood Park hinting at an exit.

The games were coming thick and fast. We hired another minibus for the trip to Bolton and Wanderers' shiny new Reebok stadium. Just as well we had received directions from local Hammer Steve Wells, or we would never have found it, as it shimmered on the horizon like an optical illusion. Fifteen-handed this time, we parked up in the adjacent shopping centre and hit the local pub, which had only opened a few days beforehand. We met Matt and Helen and chatted with a few Bolton fans, who, in the manner reserved solely for fans of doomed football clubs, remained chirpily optimistic.

As we climbed flight after flight of stairs to reach our seats, I wondered if the stadium was, indeed, an optical illusion, or something like a Tardis, bigger on the inside. I stood exhausted at the top of the stairs, beckoning the St John's ambulance man to give me oxygen. No chance. Left a bit dizzy by the height, the game started at a gentle pace. Nothing much seemed to happen and it was totally out of context when Hartson clattered into Per Frandsen with his elbow to get himself sent off.

As often happens in such circumstances, the 10 men outplayed the 11, Berkovic sliding a perfect ball through for Sinclair to open the scoring. Eyal was starting to get on my nerves. Throughout the game, he had almost snobbishly refused to pass to Lazaridis, who was working his nuts off out on the left wing, but receiving no reward for his efforts. Eyal's frustration at his less talented colleague manifested itself in a ticking off when the likeable Aussie blasted a chance over the bar from way out, attempting to re-create his spectacular effort at St James's Park.

I smiled inwardly as Berkovic spurned the opportunity to square a ball to Stan and tried to score himself. The ball was cleared, Gunlaugsson raced up the other end and crossed for Nathan Blake to equalise.

If I had been Stan, I might have chosen a few careful words for our little Israeli friend. But being the nice guy that he is, Stan just cursed and got on with the game. Two points wasted.

It seemed that no sooner had I got home, than it was time to go back to the north-west. Once again I hired a vehicle, a brand new Mondeo, to save wear and tear on my own car. I picked up Kev, Matt and Darren, before going on to Hertfordshire to pick up Buzz. To our dismay, Buzz was standing there with his brother Tom. Serious breakdown in communications. No one had told me Tom was coming and I'd allowed The Tortoise to take what I thought was the spare seat. We didn't really have time to debate the issue, it was getting on for 4pm and we had to move it. Buzz dashed inside to grab his keys, promptly locking them in the boot of his car and having to arrange temporary cover on his parents' car, so he could drive that!

The delay and diversion meant we were facing a struggle to reach Blackburn in time for kick-off. We hit the M6 at Birmingham at precisely the time we didn't want to and it took well over an hour to get through the traffic jam. I had an hour and a bit to get to Blackburn from Birmingham, so I drove seriously. What the heck? It wasn't my car. Averaging 100mph on the M6, and flicking arrogant 'V's at the flashing speed cameras, we parked up, bought programmes and perched bums on seats just as the match was kicking off. With luck like that, maybe we were in with a shout.

Berkovic was receiving some serious abuse from sections of the Blackburn crowd, reacting to the incident in the first game that had seen Kevin Gallacher sent off. Some of this hostility was race-motivated, very unpleasant, the sort of thing West Ham fans have been accused of in the past. Still, Blackburn fans went on to win the fair play award at the end of the season, so it must be worse elsewhere.

It seemed to be affecting Eyal's game. Somehow it was still 0-0 at half-time. Harry made a change soon after the break, bringing on Abou for a very out of sorts Berkovic. Suddenly we looked a different side, stroking the ball about, keeping possession, and creating a number of good opportunities. The match drifted into extra time, when Hartson scored from a move, which probably should have been a penalty anyway. We went ballistic. We looked good enough to win the game in extra time but in the second period, Ripley repeated his Christmas party trick and a penalty shoot-out beckoned – the first ever for West Ham in a major competition.

I wasn't confident. Having finished the stronger team, we might mentally have felt we should already be through. Penalty competitions are, after all, all in the mind.

It can only have taken 10 minutes, but it was one of the most dramatic 10 minutes I have ever witnessed as a West Ham fan. First Hartson, then Unsworth, Lampard and Ian Pearce equalised successful strikes from Rovers players. Pat Butcher look-a-like, Colin Hendry, who had been a rock in the Blackburn defence all night, cruelly missed their fifth, leaving Lomas to step up to bang in the winner and more than make up for the disappointment of his last trip to Ewood Park.

Understandably, we went bonkers and our celebrations spilled out onto the streets afterwards in such a way that we were, in hindsight, fortunate to escape a kicking. I drove back at a somewhat more leisurely pace, delivering the car back to the hire company the next morning and fully expecting fixed penalty notices to follow. They never showed and for that reason alone I had no hesitation in nominating the trip as the best of the season.

With a quarter-final at Highbury to look forward to, it was just like 1975. I was going back to where it all began.

36. Big Mistake

West Ham United 1 Arsenal 1 (aet) 17.3.98

March would be remembered as the month of the Arse. A month in which, over 90 minutes, we never actually lost to them, but which, ultimately left us with just one Premiership point to look positively on.

The home league match had been moved to the Monday night by Uncle Rupert. Arsenal looked nothing like the side that destroyed us 4-0 in Black September but to be fair, we didn't play to our potential either. French 'keeper Lama came in for his debut and made some good stops, while Alex Manninger, enjoying an impressive spell in the Arsenal goal, kept out efforts from Hartson and Berkovic with the aid of his woodwork.

The biggie was the following Sunday. History in recent cup-ties at Highbury was on our side and we would need all the help we could get. Pearce, after making a shaky debut, was turning into a fine purchase. His confidence was on a high and he was playing some sparkling football at the back, at times putting Rio in the shade. He put us ahead in the first half and we all celebrated, somewhat half-heartedly, and justifiably so. Within minutes, Pearce upended Keown in our box and Bergkamp levelled from the spot. Arsenal couldn't find any rhythm, though, and we were always unlikely to score more than once at Highbury, so a draw, and a replay at Upton Park, was not a disaster by any means.

After the final whistle, Vieira aimed a kick at Moncur, which should have seen him sent off, but was mysteriously missed by everyone. Funny that. Had it been the other way around, I think we might have seen more of it, or am I just being too cynical?

We were taking on the big boys and living with them. After winning, albeit on penalties, at Ewood Park, we had drawn twice with Champions-elect Arsenal, and Manchester United and Chelsea were next at Upton Park. Home matches against United are rarely dull and this proved to be no exception. We tore into them, unlucky only to have a 1-0 half-time advantage, courtesy of a scrambled effort from Sinclair. Schmeichel was at his absolute peak, tipping a fierce drive from Lampard onto the post, and a win looked odds-on. Scholes equalised for United but West Ham pushed on.

Abou scooped one over from almost on the goal line, when it surely would have been easier to score. The frustration at only drawing 1-1 was almost tangible and the required target for Europe appeared to be slipping away. Chelsea did provide us with three points, though, Hartson – still serving his suspension for his sending off at Bolton – making way for Ian Bishop, who came in for his first – and last – game of the season. Ultimately it was also his last for West Ham, as he was transferred shortly afterwards to Manchester City from whence he came.

Chelsea took a second half lead but we didn't panic. Always fragile defensively, despite their multi-million pound international players, Sinclair and Unsworth took advantage to wrap up the three points and put us in the right frame of mind for the Arsenal match.

To say we were confident was an understatement. Looking back on it now, I can see how foolish it was to feel that way. It is a recurring theme that when you expect West Ham to come up with the goods, they let you down horribly. It is perhaps unfair, on this occasion, to say that the Hammers let us down. The 120 minutes were characterised by monumental effort from both teams, played in an electric atmosphere unique to Upton Park.

We *were* confident, though. So much so, The Tortoise had booked a table at the local Indian restaurant for the post-match celebration. We reasoned this would not be a jinx, because we would celebrate whatever the result. Yeah, right.

When I look back on it now, it is like remembering a week, or maybe a month of your life, not just two hours. Stuart, the QPR fan, phoned to wish us luck. Everyone I knew who wasn't an Arsenal fan wanted us to win. Even God, I thought, who must be a neutral, would be on our side.

The first meaningful action saw Bergkamp sent off for elbowing Lomas in the face and giving him a bloody nose. We knew we shouldn't get too excited, as everyone knows 10 men can perform heroics, but Arsenal had lost their star man and that *had* to be a positive factor.

We hadn't counted on their other star man though. Nicolas Anelka scored just before half-time with a stunning strike. Literally, a stunning strike. It sent three-and-a-half sides of Upton Park into an eerie silence, the only sound to be heard being a collective muttering of "Oh f*@k."

We knew it would be a struggle now. Arsenal, famous for defending a lead, and West Ham, not exactly famous for scoring against Arsenal. Half-time came and a chance to re-group. The second half flew by and the Gooners just soaked up everything that came at them. Frustration was at an all time high, when Hartson hit the goal that sent Upton Park delirious. He dived into the Chicken Run head first, with the look of a man who felt he had effectively won the game for West Ham. Hartson had taken a lot of stick for his performances against his former colleagues, so to score a goal of this importance, at this stage of the game, must have meant a lot to him.

It meant a lot to us, too. With Arsenal's 10 men out on their feet, surely we were favourites to win the match in extra time. Lee Dixon was breathing through his arse even before the 90 minutes were up. But try as we might, we couldn't break them down again. No problem, we thought. This penalty shootout lark was a doddle. If we could do it in the hostile surroundings of Ewood Park, surely we could do it in front of our own adoring fans.

The quintet was different this time, though. Hartson turned from hero to zero in the space of half-an-hour, missing his penalty. Berkovic, too, missed his kick, but it didn't matter as Arsenal missed twice as well. Into sudden death and Adams scraped one into the bottom corner. The tension was unbearable. Our first sudden death kick came from Samassi Abou, who struck the post, and sent a dagger through the hearts of the West Ham faithful.

It's always easy to pick your penalty takers with 20-20 hindsight, but here was a man who couldn't score from half a yard, let alone 12. It seemed Abou could only score if he back-heeled it, or ran on to a flick from Moncur. None of this was debated as we walked back down the Barking Road in absolute silence. No one spoke. Devastation is an over-used word but that was how we felt. I even had tears in my eyes, I was so upset. We walked straight past the Indian restaurant we'd booked and didn't speak to each other for days.

Those of you who were there that night will relate to what I am saying. In football parlance: "Brian, I was gutted."

We hadn't really overcome the disappointment by the time Leeds United came to Upton Park for Uncle Rupert's cameras after a break for international matches. The break probably did the team the world of good and they looked fresh and eager as Leeds were beaten 3-0. It had been years since we had beaten the Yorkshiremen so this was of particular comfort, given the grieving process we were all going through. Ian Pearce was excellent once again, scoring the third and opening his league account for West Ham. He had seen an almost identical effort cleared off the line in the first half and I was pleased for him. Hartson scored the opener with a simple side-foot and Abou grabbed the second after a calamitous mistake by Nigel Martyn presented him with an open goal. Eighteen yards out, even Abou couldn't miss an open goal. It was almost the last thing he ever did as he larged it in front of the Leeds fans but other celebrating players shepherded him to safety, so he lived to score another day.

After the game, the plane carrying the Leeds United players crash-landed on take off at Stansted airport. No one was hurt but it put the importance of winning and losing into perspective for me, and made me realise I'd been a little foolish to be on the edge of tears and so grumpy after losing to the Gooners. Football is only a game, after all. And as Boris Becker once said: "Nobody died."

But even so, I still hate Arsenal with a passion.

37. It's Like That

West Ham United 2 Southampton 4   25.4.98

I think it was T.S. Eliot who said that April was the cruellest month. It certainly was for West Ham, a month that yielded only one victory and five points from a possible 15 in a run that would ultimately cost us a place in Europe.

Personally I wasn't too disappointed. I didn't think we were ready for Europe and Europe certainly wasn't ready for us. The mere fact we were even thinking about it was a bonus in my eyes.

Aston Villa were on a roll under new manager John Gregory and had come steaming up the table. We faced them at Villa Park secure in the knowledge our recent form there was good and that we had already turned them over twice that season. Stuart, the QPR fan, has a theory, however, that you never beat a team three times in a season, and he's about right with that assumption. Even Arsenal couldn't do that to us. We could justifiably expect a point from Villa Park, though, especially after we more than matched them in the first half, grazing the post and bar in the process. Our good away form deserted us, however, and Villa won the game with two late goals. The first took a massive deflection and saw Gregory leap on to the pitch like he had a firecracker up his arse. Away form may have gone but we still had our home form, or so we thought.

Derby County arrived also scrapping for a European spot. Scrapping was the operative word in a niggly match that saw Hartson fall for Igor Stimac's wind-up tactics, throwing a punch at him as they both fell to the ground. This made me question Hartson's professionalism and sanity, as he committed the foul right under the nose of the linesman and was sent packing once again. Derby had a player sent off shortly afterwards and the game degenerated into a typical April bore draw.

Brita had come down for the match and far be it from me to say she's a jinx... well. Her previous visits had seen us washed out against Newcastle United, the re-match finish 0-0 and a stuttering 2-1 cup win over part-timers Emley. Draw your own conclusions. After the game we went to The Boleyn, where we bumped into Perry Fenwick and enjoyed an anorak-type West Ham trivia session. A young lad, spotting Perry as a famous actor, came up and asked him for his autograph. As I was with him, he assumed I must be famous, too, and asked me for mine!

On Easter Monday, with Lucy sunning herself in Tenerife, we had no stopover in Sheffield. Probably just as well, as we sat in the lounge bar of the Sportsman and watched snow falling outside. It was bitterly cold, even by Yorkshire standards, and we chattered our way through another dull game in which Berkovic gave us the lead, only for Jim Magilton to equalise in the second half.

We had two strange experiences on the way home. Firstly, it was Easter and *snowing*. Bizarre. Secondly, listening to Blackburn Rovers v Arsenal on the radio and actually wanting Arsenal to win. Very bizarre. Arsenal did win, 4-1, a victory that confirmed their own title ambitions and signalled a decline for Blackburn Rovers, which would not be halted. Certainly it didn't halt the following Saturday as they arrived at Upton Park to face John Hartson making his final appearance of the season. The FA decided his red card against Derby had come too soon after his dismissal at Bolton and slapped a five-match ban on him.

He left us with two goals to remember him by, taking his Premiership total for the season to 15 and his overall total to 24. Michael Owen and Andy Cole would score more than him but had Hartson not spent nine games in the stand through suspension, one wonders what he might have achieved.

Blackburn Rovers were beaten 2-1 and it seemed the UEFA Cup campaign was back on track, but we hadn't reckoned on Southampton coming to Upton Park and stunning us with a 4-2 win. Our only double reverse of the season – against Southampton. I could not hide my embarrassment but you had to say they deserved it, Le Tissier and Ostenstad scoring goals of pure quality. With Hartson suspended and Kitson only half-fit on the bench, we relied on strikes from Sinclair and Lomas, which proved insufficient.

Still, all was not lost, as the next game was an easy away trip to Anfield. Gary had run the London Marathon the weekend before and bleached his hair blond so he would be easy to spot in the crowd. He was certainly easy to spot as we met in the car park at Goodison. The match had an air of a 5-0 drubbing about it. We were not to be disappointed. We would have to wait yet another year or three for that victory at Anfield.

Michael Owen ran through our defence like it wasn't there and we played in the style of a team that knew Europe was a bridge too far. That lackadaisical approach was mirrored in a 3-3 draw at Crystal Palace. Despite going ahead through a Lampard bobbler, originally credited as a Curcic O.G., we conspired to collapse to a 3-1 deficit, to a team that had won only once at home all season and had been relegated weeks beforehand. No matter, youth team player Emmanuel

Omoyimni, better known to his mates as 'Manny' for some obscure reason, came on as a substitute and scored twice to save our blushes and give us a mathematical possibility of a European spot. Seventh place would be enough if Chelsea won the Cup Winners' Cup.

To give us that chance we needed to beat Leicester City at Upton Park on the final day, and hope Villa lost to Arsenal or Blackburn Rovers lost to Newcastle United. On paper it looked like Arsenal – six days before the FA Cup final – might do us a favour by beating Villa but they had already won the title and had taken their foot off the gas in spectacular fashion in midweek, crashing 3-1 at Anfield. And anyway, when did Arsenal ever do us a favour?

I was completing my own personal marathon during the game against Leicester. I had attended every single match in league and cups and was frankly exhausted mentally and physically. Leicester's arrival normally ends in victory for the Irons but they still had a sniff of Europe themselves and Tony Cottee in their side – a man who often scored against his former colleagues. Lampard and Abou put us 2-0 ahead before Heskey pulled one back. Fortunes swayed back and forth, as attentions swung from the action on the pitch to the action at Villa Park, to the action at Ewood Park. Abou made it 3-1, Cottee made it 3-2, Sinclair made it 4-2 and Cottee finished the scoring to end the game 4-3.

A fitting finale to an entertaining season. We were waiting anxiously to see if seventh spot had been secured but the transistor radios buzzed bad news. Rovers had beaten Newcastle 1-0 and Villa had beaten Arsenal by the same score.

Bloody Arsenal, don't you just hate them?

38. Vindaloo

England 2 Colombia 0   26.6.98

I collapsed in a big heap and reflected on my achievement. I had now done every game in a season twice and to be honest, I didn't see it as that big a deal. I didn't feel I had to proved my loyalty to the club. If anything, I felt they owed me something, but instead season ticket prices went up through the roof again and I felt a barrier building between myself and the club I adored.

It was inevitable it would happen I suppose. With the millions of pounds flowing into the game, the big money signings, the saturation coverage on TV and the gentrification of the fan base, I wondered what had happened to the West Ham I used to know and love. Deep down I knew that without these changes, we would not survive at the top level, but the traditionalist in me still didn't like it. The mug in me still renewed my season tickets, both home and away, but I had come to realise that football was merely filling a void in my life. A void which I really wanted to be filled by a family life. See? I am a traditionalist at heart. I knew there would always be someone to fill my seat at Upton Park long after I stopped going. It was comforting in some ways, to know the club would probably always survive, but in others it was belittling to know that at the end of it all, while West Ham meant the world to me, the club didn't even know my name.

England's World Cup campaign got off to a steady

start for once, with a 2-0 win over Morocco. Rio had made the squad but his squad number of 21 said it all. He wasn't going to get a kick no matter how desperate Hoddle was. I celebrated my 30th birthday on the day we lost 2-1 to Romania. I watched the game in a pub in Canterbury, where I got chatting to a really nice girl called Jo. There was a group of four or five of us and after the disappointment of losing to a last minute goal from Dan Petrescu, we went for a last-minute kebab and, I hoped, a last minute fumble with Jo. In the end, I am told, neither materialised, as I awoke on the floor of some nearby student digs, blissfully unaware of anything that had happened from midnight onwards.

The fantasy football syndicate that met before the England v Holland game in 1996 had the foresight to book the restaurant Football Football in the Haymarket for our 1998 gathering. We weren't to know it at the time but it was also the night of England's final group match of France 98, against Colombia. The atmosphere was electric in the restaurant as the match was shown on big screens and England raced into a 2-0 lead. The joy and excitement of England getting through to the second phase was spoilt somewhat as, in fine English hooligan tradition, drinks were thrown around, followed by the buckets of water used to cool the beer. The people on the next table naturally took exception to this, and ketchup came flying back in the other direction. It was all a bit pathetic and got to the point where we were discussing dry cleaning bills, when a simple smack in the mouth would have sufficed. In the end we ran for it. 'H', Paddington, Don and Keith, the Welsh Manc, helped me and Kev to totally confuse all the American tourists pouring out of Her Majesty's after watching Phantom. I doubt they had ever seen anything like it, as we skipped merrily past, singing *Vindaloo* at the tops of our voices.

We went to Trafalgar Square to sample the

atmosphere and within minutes I found myself being hauled up onto one of the lions, posing for national press photographers. I wondered why. After all, I couldn't really give a toss about the English national side but I got swept along in the emotion of it all. I soon realised what a long way down it is from those lions. Wearing shoes with no grip whatsoever, I landed on my arse, much to the amusement of everyone around. I woke up recalling very little except for my sore bum. If you have ever been to Corfu, you will know that can be a very worrying experience.

England went out, of course, in a manner well documented elsewhere. Much to the relief of The Tortoise, who was due to marry Gail on Saturday July 4. Had England beaten Argentina that evening, we would have been playing Holland in the quarter-finals on that very afternoon. It's amazing to think how football rules our lives but had England been playing that Saturday, Darren could well still be a single man.

I couldn't stick around for the evening reception as I had stag night duties to perform in Peterborough. Stuart, the QPR fan, and Jill had decided to tie the knot and I had the honour and privilege of being his best man. In the end it was a quiet affair, five of us drinking tequila in private celebration of Croatia destroying the Germans, dancing the night away, and threatening a taxi driver with ridicule if he didn't risk life and license by taking all five of us home together.

For the wedding itself I had asked Stuart's beloved QPR for a message I could read out with my speech and, to my delight, they faxed me back a short letter inviting them both to watch a game from the executive box and meet the players afterwards. It was a nice touch, one that I doubt many other clubs would offer to their most loyal followers. My holiday that year consisted of Stuart, the QPR fan's, wedding, then a few days catching up with Lucy in Sheffield, before the serious stuff started all over again.

39. To The Moon And Back

Sheffield Wednesday 0 West Ham United 1 15.8.98

The summer saw the inevitable comings and goings –
but this time not just on the pitch. We found a shirt
sponsor at last, Dr Martens somewhat appropriately
filling the void left by Dagenham Motors 12 months
earlier. The World Cup had thrown some interesting
names into the hat. Top of the pile was Chilean Javier
Margas, who joined in a deal worth around £2.2m, the
first South American to sign for the club. Shaka Hislop,
Newcastle United's out of favour goalkeeper, also joined
on a free transfer, while Neil Ruddock eventually arrived
from Liverpool after protracted negotiations. The biggest
name, and mouth, to join was that of Ian Wright, who
came from Arsenal for an estimated £750,000.

Say what you like about Wright, to me, he remains to
this day one of the most arrogant and irritating people
ever to have walked the earth. I really didn't want to see
him in a West Ham shirt. They say when that kind of
arrogance is on your side, you change your view, but
he's chipped from the same stone as Paul Ince and I
didn't want him at my club.

David Unsworth obviously felt the same. Claiming
homesickness, he moved to Aston Villa, with only the
female supporters sorry to see him go.

I was selective in my choice of pre-season friendlies,
meeting up with Brita once again to take in the game at
Leyton Orient. West Ham came back from 2-0 down to
win 4-2, Brita got some top pics of Frank Lampard's legs

and we all went home happy.

The opening day of the season saw an expectant travelling army head up the M1 for the second year running, this time stopping just short of Barnsley and paying a visit to Sheffield Wednesday. Like last year, our opening day opponents were managed by Danny Wilson, who we had earlier cut up on the A61 making gestures at him, suggesting Wednesday were not all that good.

Sheffield was a place starting to work its way into my affections. I always had a good time whenever I went there and the combination of city life, together with the relaxed atmosphere provided by a place anywhere other than London, was appealing to me. I must admit I succumbed that night to the Ian Wright euphoria. As he scored the 85th minute winner on his debut, I found myself chalking his name up on the blackboard in O'Neills, and publicly acclaiming him in OLAS. I must have been mad. Writing his name on the blackboard was really an exercise to wind up any Wednesday fans that were in, and naturally, several other comments were inserted beneath his name before we moved to a club later on.

Another man high on the hate list was David Beckham. After his escapades that saw him sent off in the Argentina game, he had been portrayed in many sections of the press as a national villain, who had seriously let down his country. Unfortunately for him, Manchester United's first match of the season away from the sanctuary of Old Trafford was at the traditional bear pit of . . . Upton Park.

In my view, the press were to blame for a lot of the bad feeling. In a very tasteless piece of 'journalism', one tabloid printed a picture of an effigy of Beckham hanging by his neck from the main gates of Upton Park. Any intelligent person could have seen this was a set-up and it dragged the already tarnished name of the club through the mud once again.

Many people say the acidity of the vitriol directed at Beckham is motivated by jealousy. Here is a good looking young man with millions of pounds to his name, playing for the most glamorous football club in Europe, possibly the world, married to a pop icon in the skinny shape of Posh Spice.

I couldn't disagree more. Personally, you couldn't pay me enough to play for that shit-heap of a club and I've slept with much better-looking women than Posh Spice. They could sing better than her, too. The only thing he has, which I wouldn't mind having, is his dosh, and I dare say that doesn't make him very happy.

Well, the press got their way and he was ritually abused at Upton Park. Treatment he didn't really deserve but we are dealing with the football crowd mentality here, and since when did that ever follow any logic? It's just a shame that someone like Beckham earns more in a week than I do in a year, just because he can do great things with a football. But that's hardly his fault, is it? I dare say he'd still be playing football if they earned only £300 a week. Let's face it, he's not cut out to do anything else. I seriously doubt if he would be married to Posh Spice, though.

The game? Oh, that finished 0-0.

Another goalless draw followed at Highfield Road. Wright missed an easy chance but Coventry City also looked sharp, so I was pleased with a point. The ridiculous spectacle of me and Kev following each other up the motorway in otherwise empty cars was an indication of the way things had been heading on away days. Home matches had a long established pattern, meeting in The Millers for a few beers, then wandering down the Barking Road and going our own separate ways afterwards. Away matches used to be similar, but with neither Kev nor I writing regularly for OLAS any more, we were travelling away with the possé less and less.

Having been through the stage of interviewing players after the game, it now had a pretty much 'old hat' feel to it. That may sound a flippant thing to say from a man who has enjoyed the privilege. But believe me, once you have been there, you soon realise that very few of the players love the club for anything other than the pay packet they get on a Friday, while even fewer are articulate enough to have anything worthwhile to say about it.

Kev and I reasoned, therefore, that time could be more profitably spent getting home, which meant making our own arrangements. If we had separate plans after a trip, that meant travelling on our own. It was farcical, but it was the way things had evolved.

We reached the August Bank Holiday without conceding a goal and with five points in the bag from three games. Okay, we'd only scored one goal but if you weren't conceding, that wasn't a problem. With plenty of quality strikers around, surely the goals would come.

40. One For Sorrow

West Ham United 3 Wimbledon 4 9.9.98

The goals did come, for and against. It seemed all the players had a train to catch and wanted Wimbledon out of the way as soon as possible, as we raced into a 3-0 lead inside 30 minutes. Most of them must have caught that train at half time, as Wimbledon pulled themselves up by their bootlaces to win the game 4-3.

It was one of the most unprofessional displays I had ever witnessed. Had we learned nothing from Arsenal the previous season? I walked away from the game, with nephew Mark, bitterly disappointed with the way we had surrendered a winning lead. Not just a one-goal lead, but a three-goal lead. It was inconceivable, and something no West Ham side had ever done in my time as a fan.

The sloppy way we had played in the last hour of the game did not bode well for the visit of Liverpool, who came to Upton Park as table-toppers. Yet West Ham did it again, surprising everyone by inflicting Liverpool's first defeat of the season. The same score and the same scorers as the year before, Hartson and Berkovic putting West Ham 2-0 up, before Riedle exposed our inability to defend once again by pulling one back. We held on this time, though, and rightfully so. For it to happen once was unfortunate. To let it happen again would have been careless.

A trip to Northampton Town in the newly-christened Worthington Cup shouldn't have provided too much of a problem. But this is West Ham. Despite fielding a virtually full strength side, we were turned over 2-0 in one of the most embarrassing results for many a year. Sure, it was only the first leg, and yes, maybe we did have a goal disallowed which shouldn't have been, and yes, maybe we should have had a penalty. But there are only so many excuses you can make. At the end of 90 minutes, we weren't good enough to beat Northampton.

More motorway miles were clocked up as a rare event occurred, Kev missing a game as he was on best man duty in Edinburgh. Back up the M1 again to Nottingham and another limp display in front of goal ended in a third 0-0 of the campaign and a worrying lack of goals.

I visited Christina after the game. We enjoyed a nice Italian meal and went to see Lethal Weapon 4 at the cinema, before returning home to find her ex-boyfriend stalking around, tapping on the windows and generally being a menace. Unfortunately he had nothing to be jealous of, but I arranged to go back in a few weeks and go to The Goose Fair, something I had wanted to do for ages, then meet up with Stuart, the QPR fan, Jill, Mike and Nicola to see Neil Finn in concert. That's Neil Finn who used to be in Crowded House, not Neil Finn who played in goal for West Ham on New Year's Day 1996. But I'm sure you knew that. It would mean missing our annual defeat at Ewood Park but, on balance, I felt a weekend with Christina would be more enjoyable than seeing West Ham get spanked by relegation fodder.

Northampton Town returned to Upton Park and completed the job. Although we won the game 1-0 with a late strike from Lampard, it was too little, too late. Yet another exit to lower division minnows. I wasn't sure if I preferred that to losing to Arsenal in the quarter-finals. At least the expectation level wasn't so high, but the embarrassment factor more than made up for that.

Julian Dicks made a hero's return but looked a

shadow of the player he had been before his lengthy knee injury. His presence on the pitch was an inspiration, to us, if not the other players, who played like a bunch of useless twats.

The month ended with a home match against a Southampton side looking for their first win of the season. It seemed set up for a Saints victory but Wright at last managed to find the net again in a 1-0 win. In the post-goal celebrations, Wright and Ruddock parodied the recent incident at Hillsborough, where Wednesday striker Paolo Di Canio was sent off, then pushed referee Paul Alcock to the floor.

How we laughed, certain in the knowledge that we would never have someone so hot-headed playing for *our* team. Never.

I decided to miss my first match for two years. It was a hard decision but made a lot easier by the fact it was Blackburn Rovers away. The knowledge I had a buyer for my ticket, and the prospect of an afternoon spent in the company of Christina, followed by an evening with her, Stuart, the QPR fan, et al, also made the decision process simple.

I spent the afternoon at The Goose Fair with Christina – a bit of a disappointment, because, to me, it was just like any other fair I had ever been to, only with louder, more throbbing music. As we left to go and meet Stuart, the QPR fan, I called Kev on his mobile to find out the score. I hoped against hope we may have secured a win against a very ordinary Blackburn side. A point would have been better than nothing. But what did we get? A 3-0 stuffing, that's what. Well, it was Blackburn I suppose. It seems we only ever played well at Ewood Park when Blackburn were top of the league. That's not likely to happen again for a long time.

The disappointment of the defeat at Blackburn, losing ground on the top six, was tempered by a brilliant evening being entertained by Neil Finn. Not personally, you understand, but along with the other folks crammed into the Nottingham Playhouse theatre.

Realising Kev, Buzz and Tom would still be heading home down the M1, I began to think that maybe, just maybe, there was more to life than football.

41. Rollercoaster

Charlton Athletic 4 West Ham United 2   24.10.98

Aston Villa arrived at Upton Park as table-toppers and playing with a style and swagger that suggested great things for them. With our impressive home form, an exciting game was promised, so what else could it be but 0-0?

The visit to The Valley proved much more interesting. Newly-promoted Charlton Athletic had been proving a few people wrong and had enjoyed a brief stay at the top of the Premiership after a 5-0 win over Southampton. The weather was appalling. Torrential rain poured from a black South London sky as I met Kev in Bexleyheath and drove us down to The Valley for midday. Past experience told me that to get a seat in The Antigallican, you had to be there that early. As we sat there chatting with fellow Hammers fans, there was a sign of things to come. I dropped my mini radio into my pint of beer. I should have gone home there and then but instead braved the rain and watched an exciting game ebb and flow.

Ian Wright forced an own goal to put us 1-0 up, Charlton equalised, but Eyal Berkovic put us in at half time 2-1 ahead. Eyal had been experiencing a few problems at Upton Park. Despite being a terrific little player, he was clearly an irritating little git. John Moncur had already had a swipe at him at Stamford Bridge the previous season but the training ground incident with John Hartson will go down as one of the most embarrassing in West Ham's history.

It wouldn't have been so bad had Uncle Rupert's cameras not been there and captured the whole thing on video. Hartson's took a massive kick at Berkovic's head – and the whole world saw it a few hours later. Bust-ups in training must go on all the time – Alvin Martin's skirmish with Matthew Rush being a case in point – but this was so public it was hard not to be embarrassed by it. Hartson was still the bigger hero than Berkovic, so the writing was on the wall for the Israeli from that point.

My view was that they should both have been given one almighty slap, if only because they had dragged the name of the club through the dirt. Hartson did make the effort to celebrate with Berkovic at Charlton, but he was shrugged aside. John Boy later gave 'Berko' a kiss in public, the vision of which still makes my stomach turn. Seeing Hartson coming at you with the ball at his feet is terrifying enough. To see him coming at you with his tongue out must be horrific.

Berkovic's goal looked like it might be a valuable away win for most of the second half but a real smash and grab affair saw Danny Mills equalise and Andy Hunt put Charlton in the lead in the dying minutes. I was already half way down the Woolwich Road by the time Neil Redfearn scored the fourth from the spot – the driving rain hid my tears very well. In fact, the rain soaked me through to my skin. With only a trip to Newcastle to look forward to, I began to feel very, very depressed.

Dicks had played at left wing-back and been hopelessly outclassed by the rampaging Mills. Despite admitting publicly that this was not Dicksy's favoured position, Harry persisted in playing him there, turning another hero into a laughing stock.

The journey to St. James' Park had become less daunting than in previous years, however. With a win and a draw on our last two visits, it seemed it was now within the laws of the game to get a result there. Not only that, but the discovery of Big Luke's all-you-can-eat restaurant meant that we didn't really give a toss what the score was.

That relaxed attitude must have conveyed itself to the players. We had already missed a couple of sitters, and Stuart Pearce had been harshly sent off for elbowing Sinclair, when Wright raced toward the penalty area, ball at his feet. "Pass it!" I yelled at him. And pass it he did, with great ferocity, right into the back of the Magpies' net. It was magic. You could almost see the confidence drain out of the Newcastle players. And when Sinclair added a second, then Wright a third, it seemed a real trouncing was on the cards. Still, 3-0 away is a trouncing by anyone's standards and the Newcastle fans begrudgingly admitted afterwards they had been turned over by the better team.

The win rocketed us from 14th to eighth place in the Premiership and just went to prove what a funny old game football really is. We might have expected to win at Charlton and lose at Newcastle, but it happened the other way around.

We expected to beat Chelsea but it didn't happen due to our infamous slack defending. Neil Ruddock put us 1-0 up in the opening minutes in a game, which saw Blues striker Pierluigi Casiraghi collide with Hislop and be stretchered off with a serious knee injury, never to be seen again. Chelsea equalised right at the end and should have won the game, having dominated the midfield. It was frustrating. I know I am a mere spectator but when you feel you can see something so glaringly wrong, you wonder why the management can't see it too, and won't do something about it. Harry's persistence with the 3-5-2 formation had brought great results but his insistence on playing it at all costs, seemed to be surrendering midfield possession at times when it might have been better to revert to a simple 4-4-2. Anyway, what do I know?

I decided not to go to the home game against Leicester City. Now this *was* a big decision. First home game missed since Boxing Day 1994, I felt that once I had made the break, I would feel much better about it. I drove up to Stuart, the QPR fan's, house. I can't recall the significance of the occasion but that Friday night, accompanied by Mike and brother-in-law Gary, we got totally pissed in the Wagon and Horses. We left at about 2am, Mike narrowly avoiding a punch-up with a bloke he had merely told to "cheer up." The following morning I was not looking or feeling my best but Stuart had big plans. We were to spend the day building a greenhouse. Oh, deep joy. On a freezing cold November morning, extraordinarily hung over and with an extreme lack of hand-eye co-ordination, we attempted to build a greenhouse that wouldn't have looked out of place on The Krypton Factor. After 11 hours, we gave up, secure in the knowledge that West Ham had beaten Leicester 3-2 and QPR had triumphed at Crewe. All in all a good day's work.

My nephew, Mark, joined us the following Sunday for the trip to Derby. My appetite for the game had been refreshed following a brief absence and I had been looking forward to the game with great relish. I picked up Mark, then Kev and Buzz and we were in Derby by 1pm. With a 4pm kick-off scheduled for Uncle Rupert's cameras, we had a little time to kill. I had my football in the boot of the car, so out it came for a kickabout. It all started quite serenely. Nice crisp, pleasant passes but what fun is that? We started winding Kev up by wellying the ball over his head each time it was passed to him, and shouting: "Sorry!", making out it was an accident. Kev was not amused and decided to show us. Placing the ball carefully on the concrete surface of the car park, and with anger and hatred coursing through his veins, he took a swing at the ball, missed it, and slammed his foot square into the ground. His screams could be heard in London, as he collapsed in a heap on the floor. We pissed ourselves laughing, as good friends do on such occasions, but when he failed to get up after five minutes, we began to get a little concerned.

Kev really was in a bad way but, we thought, had suffered nothing more than a stubbed toe, so we picked him up and carried him to the pub, bought him a brandy and waited for the pain to subside. By 3.30pm, it was clear the pain wasn't going to go away and we had to help him hobble the mile or so to Pride Park, plonk him in his seat and leave him to grimace through the game.

The match was a triumph for West Ham. Harry had made comments before the match about being unhappy that Andrew Impey was to be sold to Leicester City and was therefore unavailable for selection. We danced with joy at the news and couldn't wait to see the back of the Gooner-supporting waste of space. The news didn't seem to affect the team, though, as Kitson and Hartson combined, allowing John Boy to score the opener. Kitson had a magnificent game, a personal victory for him, shutting up the Derby County fans who, finally realising he wasn't Paulo Alves, still barracked him throughout.

Marc Keller scored the goal-of -the-season, a magnificent strike from outside the box, to wrap up the points and secure sixth spot. Kev left with 15 minutes to go, to ensure he was back at the car at the same time as us. He winced and whinged all the way home. The following morning he went to hospital for an x-ray and found he had fractured his toe. For some reason, he won't play football with us any more.

November ended with the visit of Spurs, now

managed, bizarrely, by George Graham. The fact they now had a decent manager didn't stop us beating them though, 2-1, with a couple of strikes from Sinclair. The second was a spectacular shot from the edge of the box that made the opening titles for *Match of the Day*. The win, combined with the fact that Manchester United and Arsenal were not playing until the Sunday, meant that for 24 hours at least, we were second in the Premiership behind Aston Villa. I cut out the league table from the paper the next day and it still sits on my notice board, to remind me of what can be achieved. It also serves as a reminder that had we not been so wasteful, we might have achieved even more.

42. Believe

Leeds United 4 West Ham United 0   5.12.98

Chile's finest Javier Margas made his long-awaited comeback at Elland Road. His first contribution was to serve the ball on a plate to Lee Bowyer, who scored Leeds United's opener. It was downhill from there on. Second place seemed a long way off as we drove home from a 4-0 defeat, Ruddock sent off and my car caught by a speed camera as I emerged from the Blackwall Tunnel, too keen to get home. This time I didn't get away with it. Things didn't improve the following Saturday, when Buzz and I made the trip alone to Middlesbrough to witness a 1-0 defeat that saw us slump to seventh position. Look at that. *Slump* to 7th position! At least the second half performance had been encouraging, Moncur turning on the style in front of his old mate Gazza, while Hartson hit the post. But positive away results were still few and far between.

Keller scored another of his spectacular efforts at home to Everton the following week – what was surely meant as a cross from way out on the left wing crept under the bar. Sinclair's winner in the second half was hard luck on Everton who had battled well, but we were not in a position to be charitable. If home form went, we were in serious trouble.

The traditional OLAS Christmas drink-up had, by now, degenerated into a few old soaks getting together for a few beers and a curry. Of course, we did that every week but this time we had a real excuse, and went to the curry house we had booked prior to the quarter-final defeat by Arsenal the previous March. A bit late, but they didn't seem to mind.

Arsenal reared their ugly heads again on Boxing Day, with a 1-0 defeat at Highbury. This time we were not to be outclassed. Some better finishing might have seen us share the points but Lampard's standing foot went with the goal gaping and with it went any chance of a draw.

Coventry City were beaten 2-0 at Upton Park in the final game on 1998. We didn't know it at the time, but Hartson's strike was to be his last in a West Ham shirt. The win clawed us back up to sixth but with such patchy form, Europe still seemed a distant hope. UEFA rules meant that even fifth place might not be enough, and qualification through the Intertoto Cup might be our only chance of European football in 1999.

The other way we could qualify, of course, would have been to win the FA Cup. A third round tie at home to Swansea City should have provided a foundation to build on. I spent New Year with Stuart, the QPR fan, and friends, despite being drugged up to the eyeballs fighting the flu. I followed him down the motorway as he went to the QPR v Huddersfield Town third round tie, and watched in horror as we produced a 1-1 draw with a Third Division side, knowing full well that a replay could only end in one result. The only bright spots were a long-range goal from Dicksy – the last of his career – and the debut of young Joe Cole.

Drawing with Swansea did not put us in the best frame of mind for the trip to Old Trafford. The game was live on TV courtesy of Uncle Rupert, so I decided against making the trip. What do you mean part-timer? Before the match they had been filming scenes for the forthcoming film about George Best, and I'm told West Ham fans did their bit to try and screw it up, chanting rude songs about Bestie. I found this highly amusing but for some reason United fans didn't see the funny side. The lights went out and kick-off was delayed. I'd hoped that those Far Eastern gamblers were up to their tricks again and that the match might be postponed until a time when we might be more up for it but, alas, the lights came on and we were thumped 4-1.

I just couldn't face the trip to Swansea. I knew what was going to happen. Despite knowing the outcome from the moment the final whistle went in the first match at Upton Park, I still hoped against hope that it might not, and that a fourth round tie against Derby County would be ours. No chance. West Ham and lower division teams just don't mix. We lost 1-0 and that's all I can say. At least I wouldn't have to fork out for any more cup-tie tickets – that was the only positive note. And that was stretching it.

Scott Minto signed from Benfica for £1m. Sadly, signing a player from Benfica no longer guaranteed you a Eusebio but I still felt he would be a good buy. I had admired him as a player at Charlton Athletic and Chelsea and had met his agent while I was in Barcelona, so I had a bit of background on him. I felt that despite looking far too much like Tony Blair, he would give us an extra dimension down the left side.

He made his debut at home to Sheffield Wednesday, a match which should not have provided too much of a problem for the local Boys Brigade XI, but which West Ham somehow contrived to lose 4-0. This was just silly. Minto looked wildly ineffective, and took a lot of flak, but in truth, the whole team were poor and unfortunately for Scott, it has taken him a long time to win the respect of the fans as a result. Personally, though, I like Minto and never have a problem with him being in the team.

It was clear that with confidence at an all time low, shipping goals like there was no tomorrow, and a lack of penetration up front, some drastic transfer action was called for. Wimbledon's £7.5m offer for John Hartson was just too good to turn down. While John had gone a long way to making us a top 10 side, his recent antics and loss of form had made him, and the club, something of a laughing stock. The fact that anyone was prepared to pay £7.5m for him was quite unbelievable. The fact it was Wimbledon was so outrageous, it had me checking my calendar to make sure it wasn't April 1.

The money received from the Hartson deal was spent on two players. Marc-Vivien Foé was signed from French club Lens for £4.5m to stiffen the midfield and in a remarkable coup for Harry, Paolo Di Canio was signed for what now seems a bargain £1.7m. At the time it looked like a huge risk but hindsight is, of course, a wonderful thing.

43. You Don't Know Me

West Ham United 0 Arsenal 4   6.2.99

Di Canio and Foé made their debuts at Selhurst Park in a 0-0 draw with Wimbledon. The game should have stopped the slide, with the defence playing well, a run of five consecutive away defeats halted and two new players taking their bows. Not only that, Hartson played for Wimbledon as captain and looked overweight and overpriced.

Arsenal should not then have been able to beat us 4-0 at home. It was destined to be the final game of Julian Dicks' career and nothing went right. Tim Breacker also made his final appearance in a game which heralded the end of an era. At least, it heralded the end of a losing streak, as in the next match we finally managed a win, beating Nottingham Forest 2-1. Those deadly strikers Ian Pearce and Frank Lampard scored the goals against a Forest side seemingly already doomed to relegation.

The trip to Anfield was not appetising. Liverpool had Fowler and Owen on good form and Gerard Houllier was just starting to turn the corner and produce a Liverpool side capable of challenging once again.

In best West Ham tradition, though, we produced a performance that will live long in the memory. After going 1-0 down to a Fowler goal, we not only scored a goal at Anfield (our first since 1989), but we also won a penalty in front of The Kop (haven't even bothered looking it up). Lampard scored from the spot and although Liverpool re-took the lead before half-time through Owen, West Ham were playing better than I had ever seen them play at Anfield. Lomas, at right wing-back, looked very calm and assured. Cole and Berkovic were passing the ball beautifully while Foé provided the rigidity we had been looking for in midfield. Keller came on in the second half and bent a corner in at the near post to beat James and send the travelling faithful potty.

The game stays in the memory, though, for the fact we should have won it. A few minutes from the end, Sinclair raced through in a one-on-one with the 'keeper. Substitute debutant Gavin Holligan was square of him and had the ball arrived at his feet, he could have rolled it into an empty net and gone down in Upton Park folklore as the player who gave West Ham their first win at Anfield since 1963. Sinclair either didn't see him, or saw the headlines himself, and blazed it over the bar. If we don't win at Anfield ever again, we will never come closer.

We *felt* like we had won. Just scoring two goals at Anfield was as good as a victory, and taking four points off Liverpool in a season was virtually unheard of. In the car on the way home, Paul said: "So where does this win put us?" It was a few minutes before anyone realised his *faux pas*.

After such a great performance it would have been typical of West Ham to trip up the following week at home to struggling Blackburn Rovers. Somehow we managed to avoid it, winning 2-0. Pearce scored in his second consecutive home game against his old club, and the second came from the boot of Di Canio. His first goal for West Ham, it was remarkable only for its mediocrity, a simple side-footed tap in from a Berkovic cross. His scoring record at his previous clubs had not been prolific but the man was clearly a genius and, given time, maybe he could prove that he hadn't been such a big gamble.

As sure as winter follows autumn, defeat at Southampton came along. We decided to take the train, a wise decision as it meant we were in a totally paralytic state by the time the game started and were therefore totally unable to be hurt by anything the team could throw at us. I'm told we were shocking.

The following Saturday we had to visit Stamford Bridge, where Chelsea hadn't lost all season, and with our record of only three away victories all year we were unlikely to threaten that. We tried the same trick as the week before, travelling by train and getting hammered before going to the game, to soften the blow of another mind-numbing defeat. Paul took it all a bit too seriously and was thrown out before half time for, in the words of the steward, "looking a bit pissed." Foé had a goal disallowed in the first half which raised spirits. In the second, Kitson scrambled the ball over the line, running to his adoring fans in the Lower East Stand, and the positioning of Chelsea's blue flag was once again called into question.

We had arranged, like some sort of fire drill, that in the unlikely event of a West Ham victory we would congregate after the game in The Wheatsheaf for a post-match celebration. Paul had been there since half time and already had drinks lined up for us. By the time I left, I was very, very drunk, and spent the entire journey home ringing everyone in the memory of my mobile phone (including some very bemused customers) and explaining exactly how we did it.

Di Canio doubled his West Ham tally at home to Newcastle United. It was a measure of how far we had come that the visit of Newcastle was no longer a big deal and was generally expected to yield three points. Three points duly arrived, courtesy of a Newcastle defence politely parting and allowing Di Canio to round the 'keeper and score with ease. Kitson added a second to complete a comprehensive victory. Suddenly it was four wins and a draw from six games, and fifth place. Maybe Europe wasn't such a distant dream after all.

44. Flatbeat

Aston Villa 0 West Ham United 0   2.4.99

After topping the table in December, Villa had hit freefall. Naturally we expected this run to come to a halt with the visit of the ever benevolent West Ham, especially as Uncle Rupert had brought his cameras and given us the opportunity to visit Villa Park on the evening of Good Friday. What a nice man Uncle Rupert is. The match finished 0-0, Di Canio having one struck off for being about six miles offside, but showing all the skill and brilliance we had learned to expect from him, with his deft flicks and incisive passing.

Easter Monday provided the opportunity for revenge over Charlton Athletic, who had robbed us blind in the rain at The Valley in October. Since then things had not gone well for them and they were struggling, yet still had a very real chance of staying up. Their chances of avoiding the drop improved dramatically after completing the double over us with a 1-0 win. Keller had what appeared to be a perfectly good goal disallowed in the first half, and their 'keeper, Sasa Illic, was stretchered off injured. All the indicators pointed to a West Ham win but Graham Stuart, one of those players who always seems to score against us, popped up with a headed second half winner.

The following Saturday, Matt drove us to Leicester in his posh Merc, and we found ourselves in the quite incredible position – sitting in a pub in Leicester on a Saturday lunchtime, drinking Margheuritas. I don't drink

Margheuritas when I'm on holiday, let alone when I am in Leicester. But they were on special offer, so it would have been rude to decline. Front row seats at Filbert Street are not ideal, as you are lower than pitch level, but at least it meant my sleep pattern was not disturbed as we played out a 0-0 draw. Tony Cottee looked as sharp as ever but neither side really looked capable of, or interested in, winning the match.

Against Derby County the following week, the annual "big win" arrived. A 5-1 demolition came courtesy of five different scorers, a certain Paulo Wanchope scoring for Derby. We looked awesome. It was hard to explain how we could have looked so good against Derby, yet so poor against Charlton. My only explanation for the difference was the level of desire of the visitors must have been different. Whatever it was, I wasn't complaining, knowing full well that the next game was away at White Hart Lane against a Tottenham side with a very low level of desire.

Coincidentally, it was Buzz's 30th birthday. We met in Kev's local and had a bite to eat and a couple of beers before someone spotted that double vodka and Red Bull was on special offer. I'd never tried this reasonably new tipple and, with half-an-hour or so before we had to leave, we each bought one. Then another. Then another. If you have never tried these fiendish drinks, I can highly recommend them. They slip down very easily, smell like Rowntree's jelly, make you very pissed but also very alert, with enough caffeine in each shot to keep Dracula awake for a fortnight. Buzz and his brother, Tom, had tickets in the Spurs' end with Sarah, a friend of Buzz's. Despite being a Tott, she was a great laugh, and had no hesitation in taking the piss out of me for reading a book about the origins of World War One. Well, got to pass the time on the train somehow.

Literally buzzing, we left the pub and got two cabs to

White Hart Lane. Kev and I had front row upper tier seats and watched with joy as Wrighty lobbed Ian Walker from about 40 yards, then Keller collected a wonderful through ball to catch the Totts' defence square and ping in a second. David Ginola pulled one back and even the sending off of Moncur could not dampen our spirits.

We met Buzz, Tom and Sarah outside, the boys showing great relief at finally being able to smile. We caught the bus back to The Tollgate and met up with Kev's sister, Lorraine. There were seven of us in the little group now, and we each bought a round of double vodkas and Red Bull. As if that wasn't enough, Buzz invited us back to his local in Hertfordshire to continue the celebrations. I phoned the female friend I had arranged to meet for a drink that evening to cancel. Sarah diplomatically leant over my shoulder and cooed: "Come back to bed, darling, it's cold!" That took some explaining, I can tell you. We finally got thrown out of Buzz's local at 4am, with me, very uncharacteristically, demanding to go clubbing. That's the effect Red Bull can have on you. I tried to sleep but with a year's supply of caffeine in my veins it just wasn't going to happen, so I got the train home with Matt the following morning, vowing never to touch the stuff again.

I have always considered myself to be technologically minded. I had a mobile phone, cable TV and a computer, but I had not, at that point, discovered the joys of the Internet. My brother-in-law, Alan, sold me a computer that was Internet-ready. That Sunday, I plugged it in, went online and life was never the same again.

Actually, that's not strictly true. My first impression of the Internet was that it was a place to send meaningless email to friends, and negate the need to ever buy another jazz mag. The revolution was to come a couple of weeks later.

45. Pick A Part That's New

West Ham United 1 Leeds United 5 · 1.5.99

There was an air of inevitability about losing at home to Leeds United – but not to the magnitude or the manner of the defeat. Crushed 5-1 and with three players sent off, it was one of the darkest days of the season. Having already lost 4-0 at home on two previous occasions, it was hard to see how we had managed to keep up a top six challenge. Wright, Hislop and Lomas were dismissed, with Minto, Foé, Ruddock and Di Canio booked. From the highest of Red Bull-inspired highs, we were back at bull shit-inspired rock bottom.

The trip to Everton did nothing to help. In their last home game of a season in which they had struggled, they spanked us 6-0, and we couldn't even make the excuse that we only had eight men. We had the full 11, albeit 11 men seemingly disinterested in playing in Europe the following season.

The revolution came the next day. A casual lunchtime beer in my local got me chatting to a young lady at the bar and I happened to mention I had just got onto the Internet. "Have you tried chat?" she asked me. I had no idea what she was talking about, so asked for more details. She gave me a website address to try. That evening I went home and tried it. I was on line until 4.30am. I was hooked. Chat gave me the opportunity to talk to people all over the world in real time. It was just the most amazing thing. Unless you have tried it, you would not understand. I was on the computer every night from the time I got in from work to the time my eyelids gave up the fight and forced me to go to bed. I knew at the time it wasn't good for me but I couldn't foresee just how it would affect my life.

West Ham completed their fixture programme the following Sunday. After losing 5-1 and 6-0 in their previous two games, it was perhaps typical that we should win 4-0 at home to Middlesbrough. Sporting the stylish new kit manufactured by Fila, 'Boro were simply blown away by a wonderful footballing performance. We finished the season in fifth place, our highest ever Premiership finish, and highest league placing since the days of Cottee and McAvennie in 1985-86

But it still wasn't enough to guarantee us a place in the UEFA Cup. Ironic, because finishing seventh the previous year would have been sufficient, but UEFA obviously were so desperate to keep West Ham out of Europe that as soon as we looked like finishing higher, they raised the stakes. It made me feel deflated, at a time when I should have been buzzing, and made me re-assess the whole relationship I had with the club.

I had to make a decision. Finances were not in good shape and the cost of season tickets had gone beyond what I considered to be acceptable. With more and more games on TV courtesy of Uncle Rupert, and a rapidly filling social diary, I decided to allow football to take a back seat for a year, and see what happened.

I had been talking to a few people on the Internet and had formed some very strong friendships in a very short space of time, but my life was turned on its head when I started talking to Billie.

I had discovered a UK chat room. At first I was sceptical about this, as I thought the whole point was to talk to people around the world. I soon got hooked on chatting to people in the UK, however, and the room became like a social club, where familiar faces could hang out and pass the time of day. In June I spoke to Billie (not the teenage pop star) for the first time and, suffice to say, I fell instantly and irrevocably in love with her.

Meanwhile West Ham's competitive season began again in July with a third round Intertoto Cup tie at home to FC Jokerit of Finland. Brita emailed me, excited because we were playing a Finnish team, and I too, was excited at the prospect of seeing West Ham play in Europe, albeit in a much-maligned qualifying tournament. I went to the game at Upton Park to see Kitson, who has never let us down, score the winner in a 1-0 first leg victory. Perversely, after waiting 18 years to see West Ham play in Europe, I couldn't raise the interest to go out to Finland for the second leg. Obviously money played a part, but had I been really serious I could have done it somehow. But as I recall, I didn't even sweat over the radio, but checked Teletext the following morning to see that a Lampard goal had earned us a 1-1 draw and a place in the semi-finals against FC Heerenveen of Holland.

Again, I went to the home leg, Lampard scoring in a 1-0 win, but didn't make the trip away, watching the game courtesy of Uncle Rupert in The Queens Head in Turnpike Lane, with Kev, equally surprised at his own lack of enthusiasm for making the trip. New signing Paulo Wanchope, quickly christened "Lambchop", scored to give West Ham a 2-0 aggregate success.

August had begun with the visit of friends from different corners of the earth. The Internet had certainly broadened my horizons and I was treated to visits from Australia and the USA. Perhaps it was partly this new found circle of friends that persuaded me the need for a season ticket, or to travel to Europe to watch West Ham was not so pressing, but as it turned out, I still made the first two league matches of the season. In a sad attempt to re-capture my rapidly fading youth, I bleached my hair blond and had my ear pierced.

The Premiership campaign begun unreasonably early on August 7th at home to Tottenham. We had already played four competitive matches, and our superior fitness told as we won the game 1-0 with another goal from Frank Lampard. On the Tuesday we played FC Metz at Upton Park in the first leg of the Intertoto Cup final. The rare sight of West Ham playing at home in an away strip must have confused us, as we lost 1-0, missing a penalty in the process. It was a disappointment, but as I hadn't really expected us to qualify for Europe anyway, I didn't consider it a big deal. I was on a fortnight's holiday, and had been enjoying myself away from thoughts of West Ham. Another Monday night away trip at the invitation of Uncle Rupert. We fell behind early to a Dion Dublin goal, cancelled out by a spectacular own goal by Gareth Southgate. Dublin gave Villa the lead again in the second half, and it looked like the game was up. Kev and I trudged out with a couple of minutes to go, trying to avoid the inevitable rush for the M6. As we sat in the car, the news filtered through from the radio that Trevor Sinclair had equalised in the last minute. We whooped with joy as we sped out of the car park, larging it at the departing Villa fans, who had left the stadium believing they had won. The disappointment of missing the goal was tempered somewhat by the fact we hit the M6 right away, and I was home by midnight.

The following Saturday it finally hit me that I didn't have a season ticket. With West Ham at home to Leicester, I had arranged to go to see my parents in Hastings with my housemate Mark and go to the air show at Eastbourne. It wasn't until I was standing on the pier, watching the Red Arrows thunder past, that it suddenly hit me I was missing out. I dragged dad and Mark back to the car in time for the football results to hear that West Ham had won 2-1 with goals from Wanchope and Di Canio cancelling out an opener from Emile Heskey. It had been a glorious day down on the south coast, beautifully warm with good food and company, but my heart still longed to be at Upton Park.

This, I told myself, was ridiculous. I was cutting down on my football and that was the end of the matter. I simply didn't have the cash to fund this obsession, and besides, there was Billie, I loved her with a passion. I guess it was similar to my love for West Ham, I loved them unquestioningly, but they never gave me a trophy, just the occasional stunning away win to keep me interested.

Speaking of stunning away wins, the following Tuesday, we prepared to wave Europe bye bye with a wet hankie on a sooty railway station. I watched the game with my nephew, Mark, in his local, expecting a valiant effort, but ultimate failure. West Ham stunned me again, with a breathtaking performance they won 3-1 with goals from Sinclair, Lampard and Wanchope. Metz were a decent side, and to beat them so convincingly on their own patch was no mean feat. It was a measure of how far we had come, both physically and mentally, to be able to approach a game like that and come out of it victorious.

Kev, Buzz and Matt went to Bradford City on the following Saturday, enjoying a curry at a local hostelry while I chose instead to spend the Bank Holiday with Stuart, the QPR fan. Mike and Nicola had now produced a baby boy, John, and Jill was pregnant, expecting in December. Talk was of nappies rather than goal difference. The girls were having their revenge.

Even so we still ended up watching rugby on the TV that afternoon. The football scores flashed up in the corner, telling me West Ham had won 3-0 at Bradford, with Wanchope, Di Canio and Sinclair scoring the goals. Okay, only four league games gone, but three wins and a draw from them, and a place in the first round of the UEFA Cup to look forward to.

Life was almost perfect but, as has often been the case in my life, when West Ham do well, my personal life sucks.

46. If You Tolerate This

Everton 1 West Ham United 0 19.9.99

While West Ham were beating Watford 1-0 with a clever free-kick from Di Canio, I sat in a pub garden in Slough with an Internet friend, Celina. We had been chatting online into the wee small hours, moaning about our luck, and it seemed daft not to meet up. She's a lovely person with a heart of solid gold and remains a good friend to this day.

Meanwhile the demands of television meant that our first round, first leg UEFA Cup tie against NK Osijek of Croatia had to be played on the Thursday night. A bizarre situation but when you are a guest at the party, you don't question the timing. A comprehensive 3-0 victory came courtesy of Wanchope, Di Canio and Lampard, on an evening crammed full of atmosphere that made the hairs stand up on the back of my neck. Although very different players, I could see a parallel between Wanchope, Di Canio and Lampard, and Cottee, McAvennie and Devonshire from the 80s. All three had a profound affect on the way the team played and all three often found themselves on the scoresheet.

After making a dog's breakfast of the game at Leeds United last season, Margas had gone into hiding somewhere in South America. On his return, aware that he might not be flavour of the month with the fans, he dyed his hair claret and blue in an effort to placate us. What Javier failed to comprehend, was that it was performances, not hair colour, that swayed our views.

Despite that, Margas never really got the bird from us and at least his zany hairstyle showed his heart was in the right place. He played a blinder against Osijek, so everything was forgotten.

Undefeated in the league, Kev and I made the trip to rain-soaked Goodison Park, where the atmosphere in The Stanley pub proved to be decidedly unfriendly. I decided discretion was the better part of valour and went for a walk. I quite like my facial features the way they are and don't want them rearranged by a pissed-up scouser with a broken bottle.

The match really shouldn't have been played. There was water standing on the pitch; ball and players were skidding all over the place, but we may not have complained quite so loudly had Lambchop tucked away his one-on-one chance in the first half. In the end it was vital, as Shaka made a real howler in the second half, allowing a weak shot from Francis Jeffers to run between his legs and over the line. Still, it was only one defeat from six, so nothing to worry about.

On the way home I had arranged to meet another net friend, Dawn, in Warrington, as I virtually had to pass her door to get back onto the M6. Kev had been very sceptical about my net friends but when he met Dawn he changed his tune. "She was all right," he said as we got back into the car. From him, that is a huge compliment.

The drive home took forever. Massive jams on the M6 forced me to turn around, cut across the Pennines and try my luck on the M1. That was just as bad. It took six hours to get home and made me realise that maybe there was a reason why I needed to cut down. Another 1-0 defeat followed, at Coventry City. This was a sickener. We hardly ever lost at Coventry but the combination of their impressive home form and our inability to score away in the Premiership gave them the points. To add insult to injury, Moncur was sent off. I missed the game as I was attending the wedding of a former colleague and good mate, Bob Peverett. With a social life Tara Palmer-Tomkinson would have been proud of, a little perspective had come back into my life and I began to realise that going to football was not the only way to spend a Saturday afternoon.

On the following Thursday, West Ham travelled to Osijek to play the second leg of their UEFA Cup first round tie. I watched the game on Channel 5, wishing I could be there. It was a delight to see Kitson, Foé and Ruddock score in a 3-1 win that gave us a 6-1 aggregate victory. The joy was short-lived, though, as we were paired with Romanian side Steaua Bucharest in the second round. That was going to be tough.

Arsenal were going to be tough, too. We hadn't beaten them in any fixture at Upton Park since 1987, so a win was well overdue. No longer a season ticket holder, I wasn't able to get into the game. Actually, that's not quite true. I didn't try. Serious apathy was setting in. I might get a bit of flak from the die-hards now but having missed a few games; it really didn't bother me. It seemed to me to be a much better idea to go and have Sunday lunch with Celina and Jules in Slough, than watch Arsenal (probably) beat us at Upton Park.

Of course, looking back, although the roast beef was wonderful, I wish I had made the effort, and was able to say I was there when Di Canio scored those two magnificent goals to win the game 2-1 for us. For once it was Arsenal who dominated and West Ham who won. Wonderful. I arrived home in time to watch the highlights on *Match of the Day*, and see that French lunatic Patrick Vieira spit at Neil Ruddock. Now I am sure there are many people who would like to spit at "Razor" Ruddock, but that doesn't excuse Vieira. Foe was also sent off at the end of the game to tarnish an otherwise brilliant performance.

After receiving a bye in the second round of the Worthington Cup due to our European involvement, we faced AFC Bournemouth at Upton Park in the third round. Clearly inspired by the thought of playing against their former manager's team, the Cherries proved to be tough nuts to crack but, inexplicably, despite playing lower league opposition, West Ham won 2-0 in a very professional performance. Billie called to make me smile.

The next Sunday, West Ham lost 2-0 at Middlesbrough in front of Uncle Rupert's cameras. Shaka was sent off for handling the ball outside the area but we managed to hold on until just after half-time. In fact, by that point we should have been ahead, a blatant foul on Di Canio in the penalty area failed to receive the relevant compensation, re-enforcing the notion that referees were biased, not just against West Ham in general, but against Di Canio in particular.

It wasn't the best preparation for our second round UEFA Cup tie in Romania. Kev and Matt made the trip, to a country where colour has yet to be introduced, judging by the quality of his photographs. Still, the locals seemed friendly enough, even if they did have an alarming habit of setting fire to things inside the stadium. I watched the game on TV and could see right from kick-off we were going to struggle. In the end a 2-0 defeat didn't look too bad, although an away goal would have made the return leg a much more appetising prospect.

Still hung over from the defeat in Romania, it was a tired looking West Ham side that surrendered their 100% home record to Sunderland on the Sunday. Despite having Steve Bould sent off after an incident involving Wanchope, Sunderland played well, justifying their lofty position in the Premiership, and took the lead through Kevin Phillips in the first half. An equaliser came late on, from the boot of Sinclair.

I took a full day off on the Wednesday to drive up to Liverpool with Kev, and spend the day looking around the Beatles Experience at Albert Dock. A little bit disappointing, we thought, but something that had to be done, as we are both complete Beatles fans. The game was something of a non-event, nothing much to write home about. It is, however, a fixture I will make a point of going to every year, because I want to be there when we finally do it. A player with the ludicrous name of Titi scored a first half winner and the game was effectively over from that point.

For Anfield read Elland Road – same scoreline, a 1-0 defeat with Ian Harte scoring the winner after a poor clearance from Lomas. The European dream ended on Thursday. Despite pummelling the Steaua goal we couldn't find a way through, drew the game 0-0 and went out. Valuable experience, though, and it gave us all a taste for more. Pity really, as it wasn't going to come.

We played Chelsea on yet another Sunday, although to be fair this was more and more due to the fact we had been playing in Europe on the Thursday rather than any intervention by Uncle Rupert. A bland game ended 0-0, the only excitement coming when Margas was sent off. The season was already heading into non-event territory.

47. No Matter What

West Ham United 4 Sheffield Wednesday 3 21.11.99

I watched the game against Sheffield Wednesday courtesy of Uncle Rupert and saw West Ham struggle to beat the bottom side after twice being behind and despite Wednesday having a player sent off. Life had taken a turn on its head. From being the most important thing in the world to me, suddenly I wasn't that bothered if West Ham won or lost. Sure, I wanted them to win, as I always do, but I was so wrapped up in other things, the pain of defeat didn't linger as it had done when all there was to life was West Ham. Billie saw to that. It was a sweet, sweet period of my life. The sweetest.

Liverpool came to Upton Park but I had a date with Stuart, the QPR fan, to watch Rangers play Barnsley at Loftus Road, then spend the remainder of the weekend with him and Jill.

Sinclair scored the winner against Liverpool and I nudged Stuart, the QPR fan, on hearing news of the goal. Stuart, the QPR fan, said at the time of Sinclair's transfer that we had got the bargain of the century. At the time I was sceptical but by now I not only agreed with him, but took the time to rub the fact in at every opportunity.

The following Tuesday, Uncle Rupert invited West Ham into my front room again, this time to play Birmingham City at St. Andrews in the fourth round of the Worthington Cup. The game had disaster written all over it from the very start. Dodgy cup side West Ham against lower league opposition riding high in their division, live on TV. I watched through my hands as Birmingham went 1-0 up, before a spectacular long-range effort from Lomas levelled the scores, only for Brum to go back into the lead just before half-time with an equally stunning strike from Martin Grainger.

The game looked to be up. Injury-prone debutant Gary Charles was stretchered off. With only a few minutes to go, Kitson was thrown into the mix and popped up with an equaliser to seemingly send the game into extra time. Young Joe Cole had other ideas, though, sweeping a cross from Di Canio into the net in injury time to send the travelling fans wild, and me dancing around my front room.

A quarter-final tie against Aston Villa beckoned, a mouth-watering prospect, not least because I had a couple of net friends who claimed to be Villa fans. Here was an opportunity to have some fun.

I suppose, statistically, a 0-0 draw with Spurs had to come at some stage. Whether it is coincidence that it should arrive within a year of George Graham taking over at The Lane, I can only speculate. Once again we played at Tottenham on a Monday night for Uncle Rupert. I may be doing George an injustice; the fact that Steve Lomas was sent off early on for two innocuous challenges on José Dominguez may have contributed to the 0-0 scoreline. I prefer to believe that Mr Graham and his tactic of boring the opposition into submission had something to do with it. The first 0-0 draw between West Ham and Spurs since 1923, says it all, really.

The season was unusual for many reasons. For a start, West Ham had a side to compete with the best, but being involved in Europe meant lots of Sunday matches, and being on TV a lot meant lots of Monday fixtures, too. Manchester United's much publicised withdrawal from the FA Cup to compete in the World Club Championship, and the bringing forward of the domestic third round ties to December 11, gave the season a completely distorted look. Not only that, but the Worthington Cup quarter-finals, usually played in January, were also to take place before Christmas.

In the space of five days we were to play two cup ties that could make or break our season. The farcical nature of being a West Ham fan was about to be exposed in the cruellest possible fashion.

48. That Don't Impress Me Much

Tranmere Rovers 1 West Ham United 0 11.12.99

FA Cup third round day. Usually the first Saturday in January but the powers that be, in their ultimate wisdom, decided to defy tradition and play it before Christmas. I'd never been to Prenton Park before, so was keen to make the trip, but very quickly wished I hadn't.

I travelled up with friend Kim and daughter Gemma, in close formation with the OLAS possé. Tranmere had brought stewards in from outside to help marshal people around, as a capacity crowd was expected. With kick-off fast approaching there were still a lot of people milling about in gangways looking generally lost. The stewards invited people to take the first seat that became available, rather than the one printed on their ticket. Understandably, this led to lots of heated exchanges and a lot of lost tempers. By the time everyone was comfortably seated, West Ham were 1-0 down to a goal from Nick Henry, a former tormentor from his days at Oldham.

West Ham just didn't look interested – we were out of the FA Cup before we should have even started.

On the Wednesday we had a chance for some consolation with a quarter-final tie in the Worthington Cup, at home to Aston Villa. With Kim's season ticket I watched the game from the Bobby Moore upper. I marvelled at the ineptitude of Ruddock as he tried to shepherd the ball out for a goal kick, only to allow

Merson to nick the ball off his toes and cross for Ian Taylor to open the scoring. Upton Park groaned as one. It seemed our nine-year wait for a semi-final place was to be extended.

In the second half, though, West Ham rallied and Lampard grabbed an equaliser. It looked like extra time, possibly penalties, but in the last minute Margas made a similar mistake to Ruddock, allowing Joachim to cross for Dion Dublin to score. Game over, or so we thought.

With thousands streaming out of Upton Park, Kitson raced up the other end and was tripped for a penalty. With an ice cool nerve, Di Canio chipped the ball into the bottom corner, dramatically forcing extra time.

With just seven or so minutes remaining, Manny Omoyimni, hero at Selhurst Park a couple of years before, came on as a substitute to give us a further attacking outlet. But he did nothing of note, no more goals ensued and the game went to penalties.

In one of the most dramatic penalty shootouts ever, Gareth Southgate – an extraordinary choice given his track record in these situations – saw his weak kick easily saved by Shaka and West Ham were into the semi-finals. Or so we thought.

After gloating to friends, Tony and Justin, about our marvellous victory, I received a message online on the Saturday morning from Tony, which simply said "Cheating Hammers!" Blissfully unaware of the dramatic turn of events, I sent one back saying: "You're just a bad loser!"

Seconds later my phone rang. It was Kev delivering the shocking news.

49. I Want It that Way

West Ham United 2 Manchester United 4   18.12.99

Manny Omoyimni had, it seemed, appeared twice for Gillingham in an earlier round of the Worthington Cup, while there on loan. The rules state that if you have played for another team in a cup competition, you can't play for another, and as such Manny was "cup-tied." West Ham had broken the rules. I felt a chill run down my spine as Kev explained the news. This was just so typically West Ham that I shouldn't have been surprised. In fact I wasn't surprised, I was just disappointed that it had been allowed to happen.

Naturally, we all looked for someone to blame. Should Harry have been aware? Probably not, he had enough to deal with without checking eligibility. Should the club secretary, Graham Mackrell, have been aware? Yes, probably, and he did resign over it, but it later emerged that they had sought confirmation from Gillingham that Manny hadn't played, and they had been told he hadn't. Who did we believe?

In the end, the responsibility had to end with Manny himself. He must have been aware of cup-tie rules, and known that he had played for another team in an earlier round of the same competition. That may have been the view the club took as well, as he was dumped unceremoniously on loan to Scunthorpe United and now plies his trade in the salubrious surroundings of Oxford United.

It still wasn't a disaster. We hadn't been kicked out of

the Worthington Cup – that was the worse case scenario. We could even be allowed to continue. After all, Manny had only been on the pitch for seven minutes, touched the ball once and didn't take a penalty. But Deadly Doug Ellis, the Villa chairman, wasn't going to let things rest. He wanted to see us kicked out and Villa take our place in the semi-finals. Rightly so. I'm sure, had the boot been on the other foot, we would have wanted Terry Brown to fight our corner. In the end, common sense prevailed and the tie was ordered to be replayed at Upton Park on January 11. We had another bite at the cherry.

Whether the fiasco affected the team as they took on Manchester United at Upton Park that afternoon, I cannot say. Something must have affected them, though, as West Ham went 3-0 down in the space of half-an-hour. Di Canio pulled one back before half time, then scored a brilliant second, rounding the 'keeper to slot home. The Italian maestro narrowly missed out on a hat-trick, trying to lob instead of shoot past Van Der Gouw, and from the breakaway, United scored a killer fourth. Later, different camera angles showed Paolo pummelling the ground in frustration as United's fourth went in. His obvious passion for the game endeared him to a generation. It was the end of a traumatic week for West Ham but with no more games until after Christmas, we could re-group and relax a little.

My cousin, Mel, from New Zealand, was staying for a few days, and she got me good and drunk before leaving for home just before Christmas. Another cousin, Corey, known to his friends as "Skin", joined us, and I found out to my cost exactly how much New Zealanders can drink. The taxi driver certainly found out, too.

I felt I was coming down with a touch of flu. I awoke on Christmas Eve to find my gums bleeding and swollen, and my mouth full of ulcers. I was in agony. I wouldn't normally trouble my doctor on Christmas Eve but this looked serious, so I drove down to the surgery to be told it was probably a reaction to stress, and the fact I was coming down with the flu. I was prescribed a pain killing spray for the ulcers and told to go away. I was in so much pain, Christmas Day was a nightmare. I sat pushing my dinner around on my plate, unable to eat because of the searing pain in my mouth. Mum liquidised my dinner for me. I felt awful.

I had a ticket for the Boxing Day game against Wimbledon at Selhurst Park and woke that morning feeling a little brighter, so decided to go. I had promised to feed a friend's cat in Crystal Palace on the way, and let myself in to find the place had been burgled. Terrific. The pain was coming back to me and I wasn't in the mood to deal with it, so I called another friend and asked them to sort it out. I sat through the game like a zombie, not daring to move, or shout, or even breathe. Wimbledon went a goal up after some sloppy defending at a corner but Sinclair equalised before half time, then Lampard put us 2-1 ahead. We were seemingly in possession of the three points until Shaka had other ideas, pawing the ball into the path of Neil Ardley in the dying minutes to present Wimbledon with a Christmas gift of a point they scarcely deserved.

I grimaced all the way home, partly because of the way we had blown two points, but also because the pain in my mouth was becoming worse. I looked in the mirror, and panicked, seeing my gums all swollen and bloody. I broke down in tears, fearing I might lose my teeth, possibly my best feature! Pain killers were doing nothing for me, so I had to act. I decided to go to the local accident and emergency department and see if they could help. I might as well have stayed at home. They gave me some Ibuprofen and told me to see my dentist when they opened again. Hardly satisfactory.

A third sleepless night in a row left me desperate. I called the emergency dentist and was seen right away. She immediately told me I had ulcerated gingivitis, gave me antibiotics and a mouthwash, and threw her hands up in horror at the way my doctor and the hospital had treated me. If I hadn't had a mouthful of blood I would have kissed her. The drugs she gave me brought almost instant relief from the pain, although I still found eating a problem and wouldn't be allowed to touch alcohol over the millennium celebrations.

I was too ill to go to see the last game of the 20th century, at home to Derby County. After spanking them 5-1 the year before, hopes were always going to be way too high and that proved to be the case. Di Canio scored another of his spectacular goals to equalise, but a winner could not be found.

After a very understated millennium celebration, I missed the first game of the 21st century, too. I had a ticket for it, but the prospect of travelling all the way to Newcastle while still under the weather did not fill me with joy. Certainly the prospect of all-you-can-eat-for-£5.50 at Big Luke's wasn't an incentive. Like many others that day, I let the ticket sit on the side unused. Criminal.

Naturally I was feeling a lot better by the time it came to going back to work. My doctor had suggested that maybe I was letting things get on top of me just a little, what with my work and my financial situation. This pressure and stress, she claimed, had manifested itself in my illness over Christmas, but I wasn't convinced. I had noticed, though, that I was experiencing violent mood swings depending on how life was treating me. Life was great when it was good but a real downer when it was bad. No middle ground.

Villa fans would say that justice was done at Upton Park on the night of January 11. Maybe West Ham are just destined never to win anything ever again. Who knows? Whatever the reason, we were beaten after extra time in the replayed quarter-final. Lampard put us ahead but Villa equalised and in extra time they went ahead. Despite winning a penalty, Di Canio contrived to miss it this time and Villa scored a third to knock the stuffing out of us and totally deflate and disillusion the Upton Park faithful, young and old. Same old story.

By a strange quirk of fate we faced Villa again the following Saturday in the Premiership at Upton Park. Di Canio's infamous gesture to the Villa fans summed up all our feelings, but at least we avoided defeat, just, with Di Canio scoring to earn us a 1-1 draw.

Wanchope was starting to get on everyone's tits. At the start of the season he had scored a few goals and looked a decent player but by now he was just an irritating embarrassment. Harry persisted with him, particularly away from home, which defied explanation. We needed a player who could hold the ball up but Lambchop seemed to spend most of his time giving it away or falling over. While West Ham fans with long memories will know this is a tradition at the club, it's not one that necessarily has to be perpetuated.

Lambchop proved us all wrong at Leicester City, bagging a brace in a 3-1 win, with Di Canio getting the other, but his lack of consistency was a problem. While Di Canio may not have been scoring in every game, he was always making a contribution. Lambchop could spend weeks just standing there like a lemon, then do something inspirational. With the total commitment required to play in the Premiership, for me, it wasn't enough to justify a regular place in the team.

The annual defeat at The Dell followed. In a break from normal tradition, Kev and I failed to get blind drunk but instead went shopping in Southampton. Being Glenn Hoddle's first game in charge of the Saints, it was even more obvious than usual that we would lose, but it seemed a rare point might be available if we could hang on to Lampard's equaliser. Gary Charles, quickly working his way into my All-time Useless Hammers XI, had other ideas, though, and put the ball though his own net to give Hoddle the win Eileen Drewery must have predicted would come.

The Bradford City home game has since been labelled "The Day of Reckoning" by the video producers, but it might just as easily have been more accurate to call it "The Day of Shite Defending". Neither side seemed all that bothered about winning the game, giving away goals with gay abandon. I watched the game on Teletext, which is a tricky experience at the best of times. We went 1-0 down early on, only to turn it around 2-1 with goals from Sinclair and a screamer from Moncur. Within seconds Moncs had conceded a penalty and Bradford went in at half time level at 2-2. In the second half, the player formerly known as 'Mr Pineapple Head', Jamie Lawrence, bagged two goals to embarrass young substitute 'keeper Stephen Bywater, who had been called upon to make an unexpected debut after Shaka was carried off following an early collision with Dean Saunders.

After failing to win a penalty for the second time, Di Canio got the hump and sat on his haunches near the tunnel, pleading with Harry to substitute him. It was something that had to be seen to be believed, but more was to come. We then had the embarrassing spectacle of Lampard and Di Canio squabbling over who was going to take a penalty that had finally been won by Kitson. Paolo had missed his last penalty, in the cup-tie against Villa, and Lampard wasn't prepared to let it happen again.

Di Canio, a mad glare in his eyes, wasn't going to lose the argument. He wasn't going to miss the penalty either and made it 4-3, lecturing 'Young Frank' all the way back to the centre circle.

Joe Cole scored his first Premiership goal to equalise, leaving Lampard to have the last word, after all, curling the ball into the top corner in the dying minutes to win this most bizarre game, 5-4.

50. You Needed Me

**Sheffield Wednesday 3 West Ham United 1
11.3.2000**

That was as good as it got. For West Ham, the drama of a comeback like that against Bradford City simply proved too much. Bywater's shaky performance prompted Harry to bring in Charlton's out of favour 'keeper Sasa Ilic on loan for the home game against Everton. But it proved a disastrous choice. He should have trusted the kid, as we crashed 4-0.

Like Billie, I loved West Ham dearly but could have used a little more from them at times. While they both might have let me down time after time, they never hid their true feelings for me. But while I always knew exactly where I stood with West Ham – waist high in cack. Something was going to have to give and neither my relationship with West Ham nor Billie could continue this way.

I had a net friend who lived in France by the name of Amy. She would always listen to my problems and give me advice. Ruth in Edinburgh was similarly kind and caring, Fabiana has been a staunch and loyal friend throughout the last year, Debs in Dorset and Linda in Buckie have also. I hope I have been able to be similarly loyal to them all.

Watford provided us with a rare away win. Kev had been struggling with arthritis in his neck, so I volunteered to drive us the short distance from his house to Vicarage Road. We watched Liverpool draw 1-

1 with Manchester United on a tiny screen in a back-street Watford pub before taking our positions. West Ham cruised into a 2-0 lead with goals from Lomas and Wanchope, before giving us all the usual jitters and allowing Watford to claw one back.

Kev was in a pretty bad way. He didn't even want to drink. Yeah, I know. Nephew Mark and I gratefully accepted Matt and Helen's season tickets for the midweek game at home to Southampton. We won it 2-0, Lambchop scoring again and Sinclair wrapping things up with a classy second. The league table was so tight, the win bounced us from 11th up to sixth. Now qualification for Europe was a real possibility, particularly with the fixtures on the horizon not appearing to be that difficult.

Sheffield Wednesday away, for example. Well, it didn't look too difficult. I made a rare trip with the OLAS gang to find that virtually every face, except for Gary's and Clicker Jason's, had changed. I shared the driving and was glad to be part of the OLAS experience again. I had forgotten, though, that being part of OLAS usually involved getting spanked at venues where we should easily win. Lampard put us in front at half time before it all went seriously bandy and we lost 3-1. Where I might have sulked over the Sunday in previous years, Billie made sure I didn't have time to mope..

A 0-0 draw with Chelsea followed, Igor Stimac this time being the player to get his marching orders. The same day, my cat, Ludo, died after a short illness. It might sound stupid but I felt I had lost one of my most loyal mates.

As usual, Stuart and Jill, and their new arrival Callum, were there to pick up the pieces. I am blessed with some terrific friends and although I was fighting back the tears at first that night, Stuart, Jill, Mike and Nicola soon had me laughing again, albeit only for a few hours.

West Ham put a smile back on my face too. I had Kev's season ticket for the home match against Wimbledon, as his neck was still too sore to put up with the hurly-burly of a football match. He still moans about the fact that I saw that game at his expense, for two reasons. Firstly the debut of Frederic Kanouté, a young French striker signed on loan until the end of the season from Olympique Lyonnais. He was simply outstanding. As a front player, he was everything that Lambchop wasn't. Every time the ball came to him it stuck, then he found a colleague with a decent pass. He had pace, determination and a very delicate touch for a tall man. He was clearly, we thought, too good to stay around for long.

Secondly, a wonder strike from Di Canio to open the scoring, volleying in a Sinclair cross from an acute angle. It left us all speechless and went on to become *Match of the Day's* Goal-of-the-Season. Kanouté bagged one himself, before ex-Hammer Michael Hughes scored another spectacular goal for the Dons to reduce the arrears. Not enough to take the shine off an outstanding performance, one which kept me smiling for three days.

51. You Get What You Give

Manchester United 7 West Ham United 1   1.4.2000

Disastrously, Billie decided it wasn't going to happen so, with depression hanging over me, I decided the last thing I needed was to travel to Manchester to watch my beloved West Ham ritually humiliated. I immersed myself in the friendship of Amy, Ruth, Fabiana, Stuart, the QPR fan, Jill and the love and warmth of my sisters and parents. I had invested time and love in West Ham United. And they repaid me by getting slaughtered at Old Trafford.

I watched the game on the big screens at Upton Park, having first seen the youth team dispatch their Manchester United's counterparts 5-0, with the impressive Jermain Defoe grabbing a hat-trick. When Lambchop put us 1-0 up from a Kanouté flick-on, it seemed maybe it was to be our day. But football, as we all know, has a habit of kicking you when you are down.

The final score of 7-1, though, was a bit excessive. I exchanged text messages with Matt Molloy throughout the game. They started off with: "That Wanchope – I always said he was a bit special." They ended with: "Oh bollocks!" After the game I drove to my parents' house in Hastings listening to the 606 Show on Radio Five, where some rabid Mancs had the front to criticise West Ham fans for leaving early and not showing more loyalty. That made my blood boil. I rang for 30 minutes until I got through and booked a call, doing my Mr Angry on live radio at bemused host Charlie Whelan. I said: "It's a bit rich for a United fan to call us disloyal, with all the rubbish we have to put up with away from home. If any set of fans are entitled to vote with our feet, it's ours."

I then launched into a monologue about how the ref was biased against us and how the world is just so unfair. It was just how I was feeling at that point about life in general. If the country would have listened I would have gone on to tell them about my personal life. My voice must have had a hint of desperation in it, because they selected a few of my comments to use as a trailer for the following week's show.

Out of the blue, I got a call from Amy. She was back in England after leaving her husband in France. I had given her my mobile number months earlier, so I was shocked, but pleasantly surprised, when she phoned. We arranged to go out for a drink that Sunday and instantly hit it off.

Newcastle United arrived at Upton Park with their tails between their legs following their FA Cup semi-final defeat by Chelsea the previous Sunday. They took the lead but West Ham, playing with three strikers in Di Canio, Lambchop and Kanouté, proved irresistible in the second half. Lambchop bagged a brace to grab three much needed points and leave Newcastle empty-handed on a second successive trip to London.

I returned the favour Kim and Gemma had shown in taking me to Tranmere by giving them a lift to Derby. Kev made up the numbers, his neck feeling a lot better, although I'm sure his toe gave him a few twinges as he returned to the scene of the previous season's "accident." We met Buzz and Tom in the usual pub before taking our seats for an away victory that showed lots of character after the previous trip to Old Trafford. Wanchope again scored twice against his old club in a comprehensive win in which we never looked in trouble. The only downer was a bad injury to Cole that would see him miss the rest of the season, plus an hour-long wait to get out of the car park, but that's always easier to bear in victory.

52. Witch Doctor

West Ham United 0 Leeds United 0 14.5.2000

West Ham won a third consecutive game, spanking Coventry City 5-0 at Upton Park. This was our now expected end-of-season big win and was achieved with some stylish, swashbuckling attacking play. If you squinted hard you could just about see Hurst and Peters in their prime, undoing defences at will, but just as easily getting murdered. It was reassuring to know, that even in this big money era, nothing had really changed at West Ham.

After much soul searching, I decided to write this book. It was an opportunity to get the last six years into perspective and help not just me, but hopefully you, to realise just how far West Ham have come in such a short space of time. I met with the publishers before the Middlesbrough game, then witnessed a very disappointing display in which 'Boro defended like tigers and that irritating little git Ince once again finished a game at Upton Park with a beam all over his smug face.

At Highbury we took the lead through Di Canio but inevitably gave in, Overmars and Petit scoring. Petit's winner looked highly dubious, as he appeared to control the ball with his hand. Sincs was sent off in the heated protests that followed their winning goal and our mood changed dramatically in the space of 20 minutes. It was a similar story at Sunderland, where Kevin Phillips scored the winner, and the season appeared to be ending in not so much of a roar as a whimper. With

European qualification an impossibility, it seemed the team was just going through the motions and fulfilling their contractual obligations until the serious stuff was to start again in August. We didn't even have any players on the fringes of any of the squads to take part in Euro 2000. Rio was a possibility for England but we knew, deep down, when it came to the cut, he wouldn't be there.

Leeds United were looking for a Champions' League spot when they arrived at Upton Park on the final day of the season. Although it had been a year ago, the memory of their 5-1 win was still fresh, so a battling 0-0 was, in my eyes, a good result. Not that I was worrying too much about football at this point in my life.

The previous year had taken its toll on me. After Billie, I was drained emotionally and physically, not to mention financially. Mark, my landlord, was selling up, so I was going to have to find a new place to live. My doctor had sent me for counselling and told me to change my lifestyle, pronto. I was struggling financially and hated my job. I needed to change a few things in my life. I needed a new job. I needed a new house. I needed a new career. I could change all of those things; that was within my power.

I needed to change my football team, too, but that is not something that can be physically done, and at the end of it all they still provide the only chink of light when all around is dark and depressing. Like it or not, things will always change. But it's reassuring to know that despite the fact that my beloved, greed-driven game has altered beyond recognition since the advent of the Premiership, one thing that will not change – at least I hope it won't – is that unless a bigger club come in for me, I will always be West Ham 'till I die.

Epilogue

So where are we? After all the hype surrounding the start of the 2000-01 season, West Ham currently sit anchored to the bottom with three points from six games. There can be no doubt this is a false position, and we will not be relegated, but when you make a bad start like that, it's always difficult to turn things around.

This season is perhaps a microcosm of the previous six campaigns. Words I may have used a thousand times before in this book: "When you expect something from West Ham, they let you down."

Perhaps that's a little unfair, as our opening six matches did include games against Chelsea, Manchester United, Liverpool and Spurs, which in any season might only yield two points. But when they all come at the start of a campaign, it throws shortcomings into sharp focus.

Anyone who witnessed the way we pulverised Leicester City in the opening 45 minutes of our first home league game will scratch their heads and wonder exactly how we lost it. Yet, at the time of writing, Leicester City sit joint top of the Premiership and we sit rooted to the bottom. Funny game football. Bloody hilarious.

Euro 2000 came and went and England suffered once again for relying on experience rather than youth. Too many words have been written about it for me to expand here. After all, no West Ham players were involved and the since departed Kevin Keegan became the latest coach since Ron Greenwood not to take West Ham players seriously. Perhaps if Rio, Frank Lampard and maybe even Joe Cole had been thrown in, he might now be receiving his Knighthood. We can only speculate.

Davor Suker finally joined West Ham a year after his name had first been mentioned. No doubt lured by the free transfer, and the fact his pal and compatriot Igor Stimac was already here. In the games I have seen him play I have seen a few flashes of brilliance from him, but also flashes of petulance and, dare I say it, bad sportsmanship. That's something I don't want to see at my club.

Not that it's *my* club any more. Not that it ever was. As fans we label West Ham as "our" club, but the club was here before us and it will be here long after we have all gone. The club doesn't depend on us. As long as Uncle Rupert keeps pumping the dosh in, our presence at games will be viewed by the club as a mild inconvenience rather than an absolute necessity.

When you can hear a pin drop at times during a game, you can see why. The role of the spectator has been somewhat marginalised. These days, when I go to a game, I feel I am intruding rather than being made welcome. And when, as a non-season ticket holder, I am quoted £32 for an obstructed view in the West Upper, I begin to think maybe it's time to jack it in.

To say the club needs to charge such high prices to keep top class players at Upton Park is folly. They charge high prices because they know people will pay them. It's basic supply and demand. The revenue received from TV and merchandising will keep the playing squad in mansions, jewellery and fast cars for many a year. Gate money is merely a bonus.

Yet I still find myself in possession of tickets for matches at Walsall and Coventry City. So why do I do it? Is it merely that I am a creature of habit? Or is it more deep rooted than that. It's a fact of life, that once you

238

become attached to a football club you will always love them, no matter what. If someone says they have a spare ticket and asks: "Do you want it?", you don't think twice, you take it. The fact I have bought tickets for matches recently and yet left them lying on the side at home, is neither here nor there. Life moves on and different priorities come to the fore.

For me, something has had to change, and change drastically. I applied for a job within the CIS, working in Nottingham. And to my astonishment, I got it. I have a chance for a fresh start. A new job, a new residence, a new circle of friends, while still retaining those I have loved over the years.

If you want to know the full Billie story, you'll have to come to Nottingham.

As I enjoy away games in the main more than home matches, I reasoned I would also be centrally located for trips to Derby, Leicester, Leeds, Manchester, Liverpool and Birmingham. Even Newcastle will only be two hours away.

But football must take a back seat. It has to. You will no doubt have realised it had already been fading into the background by the comparatively cursory way I have described the last two seasons. It has become a chore and like any other relationship, when it feels like an obligation rather than a pleasure, it's better to back away, to allow the old feelings to come back.

Since finding the Internet I have learned a great deal. About life, about love, and about the way people think and operate. Despite this new found understanding, there are still people I will never be able to fathom. Harry Redknapp is one of them.

Harry swings in my thoughts from "genius" to "madman" on an almost daily basis. I suppose there is a fine dividing line between the two, just as there is between love and hate. There can be no doubt, however, that Harry is the man to manage West Ham United. Even if the unthinkable were to happen and West Ham were relegated, the directors should think long and hard about disposing of him. Harry is the embodiment of everything that is good and bad about the club we love. His razor sharp wit and cunning transfer deals can be breathtaking. His tactical awareness can at times be bloody irritating. But he is the man for the job. God bless you, Harry. May you have many more years at the club (and maybe a trophy or two, please?).

As for the team, he has assembled a squad of players with a blend of youth and experience synonymous with successful sides. Whether we can hang on to them long enough to achieve anything, remains to be seen. With Di Canio, Suker, Stuart Pearce and Nigel Winterburn well into their thirties, youngsters like Joe Cole, Rio Ferdinand, Frank Lampard, Michael Carrick and Jermain Defoe can surely only learn from them and become the stars of the future. It feels like Rio and Frank have always been there anyway, yet they are both only 22. The future is, indeed, bright, but only if we can keep them together.

We might moan about the club lacking ambition at times but I can't think of a recent sale that hasn't led to an equally big purchase. Players like Slaven Bilic, who were allowed to go, clearly did not have the affinity with the club that is required. His recent bid to return was turned down on medical grounds, and he has of course now returned home to Hadjuk Split. Despite being the epitome of the mercenary foreigner, I still feel we owe him a great deal. He was a super player.

To make me look stupid, Di Canio may have gone by the time this book hits the shops but I firmly believe the future of the club lies in his hands. I think he should stay on after retirement in a coaching role. His enthusiasm and determination, which doesn't always manifest itself in the right way, can only be infectious. He comes across as a nice bloke, and a winner. Just what I believe West Ham should be all about. Winning at all costs has never been the West Ham way. And nor should it be. If you can't win by playing the game, then go down playing the game and fighting.

As for the fans, I dare say we will turn up no matter what. The demographic profile of the average West Ham fan has, without a doubt, changed since I started attending regularly in 1983. The whole experience is not how it used to be. But then, maybe I am guilty of indulging in misty-eyed nostalgia. Winning still feels terrific, while losing still hurts. But neither emotion is as intense as it used to be – not for me anyway.

West Ham are very lucky. All clubs claim to have the best supporters in the land but Hammers fans have something special about them. I am sure this derives from the fact that West Ham have never been a consistently successful club, so therefore those people who choose to support them have a different nature to those who might follow, say, Arsenal or Manchester United. Sense of humour, as a West Ham fan, and the ability to poke fun at yourself, is paramount. If you do not possess these qualities, you will either end up as an Arsenal fan or at the funny farm. Same thing, I suppose.

So what's the conclusion then? West Ham are like your favourite woman. They might piss you off from time to time and they might break your heart on occasions. But they can also make you feel on top of the world. The merest thought of them can bring a smile to your face. Your head doesn't make the choice, your heart does.

Like it or not, we'll all be West Ham 'till we die.